www.ingramcontent.com/pod-product-compliance
Lightning Source LLC
Chambersburg PA
CBHW072154200426
43209CB00052B/1197

Divine Feminine and Masculine Energy

Unlock Inner Power and Achieve True Balance

© Copyright 2024 - All rights reserved.

The content contained within this book may not be reproduced, duplicated, or transmitted without direct written permission from the author or the publisher.

Under no circumstances will any blame or legal responsibility be held against the publisher or author for any damages, reparation, or monetary loss due to the information contained within this book, either directly or indirectly.

Legal Notice:

This book is copyright-protected. It is only for personal use. You cannot amend, distribute, sell, use, quote, or paraphrase any part of the content within this book without the consent of the author or publisher.

Disclaimer Notice:

Please note the information contained within this document is for educational and entertainment purposes only. All efforts have been executed to present accurate, up-to-date, reliable, and complete information. No warranties of any kind are declared or implied. Readers acknowledge that the author is not engaging in the rendering of legal, financial, medical, or professional advice. The content within this book has been derived from various sources. Please consult a licensed professional before attempting any techniques outlined in this book.

By reading this document, the reader agrees that under no circumstances is the author responsible for any losses, direct or indirect, that are incurred as a result of the use of the information contained within this document, including, but not limited to, errors, omissions, or inaccuracies.

Your Free Gift
(only available for a limited time)

Thanks for getting this book! If you want to learn more about various spirituality topics, then join Mari Silva's community and get a free guided meditation MP3 for awakening your third eye. This guided meditation mp3 is designed to open and strengthen ones third eye so you can experience a higher state of consciousness. Simply visit the link below the image to get started.

https://spiritualityspot.com/meditation

Or, Scan the QR code!

Table of Contents

PART 1: DIVINE FEMININE ENERGY 1
    INTRODUCTION 2
    CHAPTER 1: WHAT IS THE DIVINE FEMININE? 4
    CHAPTER 2: EXPLORING THE DIVINE FEMININE ARCHETYPES 16
    CHAPTER 3: DISCOVERING THE INNER GODDESS 29
    CHAPTER 4: SACRED UNION WITHIN: BALANCING YOUR ENERGIES 41
    CHAPTER 5: YOU'RE NEVER ALONE – SPIRIT GUIDES 51
    CHAPTER 6: CONNECTING WITH YOUR ALLIES 60
    CHAPTER 7: CULTIVATING DEEPER BONDS 68
    CHAPTER 8: MEDITATIVE PATHWAYS: ACCESSING HIGHER CONSCIOUSNESS 76
    CHAPTER 9: PRAYER AS A SACRED RITUAL 84
    CHAPTER 10: A CONTINUAL SPIRAL OF GROWTH 90
    CONCLUSION 95
PART 2: SACRED MASCULINE ENERGY 97
    INTRODUCTION 98
    CHAPTER 1: WHAT IS THE SACRED MASCULINE? 100
    CHAPTER 2: THE ARCHETYPES 109
    CHAPTER 3: AWAKENING YOUR DIVINE MASCULINE ENERGY 123
    CHAPTER 4: INNER STRENGTH AND COURAGE 134
    CHAPTER 5: CLARITY OF MIND AND FOCUS 144
    CHAPTER 6: BECOMING A LEADER 155

CHAPTER 7: ENHANCING THE CONNECTION: MEDITATION 167
CHAPTER 8: FINDING THE BALANCE WITHIN 176
CHAPTER 9: TOOLS FOR HEALING MASCULINITY 185
CHAPTER 10: THE EVER-UNFOLDING PATH 197
CONCLUSION 203
HERE'S ANOTHER BOOK BY MARI SILVA THAT YOU MIGHT LIKE 206
YOUR FREE GIFT (ONLY AVAILABLE FOR A LIMITED TIME) 207
REFERENCES 208
IMAGE SOURCES 214

Part 1: Divine Feminine Energy

Unlocking the Power of the Goddess Within, Connecting with Your Spirit Guides, and Accessing Higher Consciousness through Meditation and Prayer

Introduction

For the longest time, the Divine Feminine has been suppressed. Society has worked ceaselessly night and day to ensure all knowledge of this divine energy is unavailable to anyone. However, times are changing. People are waking up. Most realize they've been sold a bunch of stories by the current establishment – an establishment perhaps desperate to ensure their perverted version of masculinity continues to thrive and suppress others.

No, *this book isn't a war on masculinity.* It's been written to help you understand your life should be full of more ease and flow than it currently is. It will show you how the world could be transformed for the better if it had a balance between creation's dual energies - the Divine Feminine and the Divine Masculine. For far too long, an imbalance has rocked the world on individual and collective levels, causing far more pain and heartbreak than anyone should bear. As you read this book, you'll discover why things are the way they are and what to do.

It all starts with you.

As each person embarks on their personal journey of reconnecting with the Divine Feminine, the world benefits from the snowball effect. More and more people are awakening to the truth of who they are meant to be, including you. You'll experience the benefits of finding a balance between both energies in your personal life and witness the effects of your choices on collective humanity.

There are many benefits to living with an awareness of the power of the Divine Feminine and allowing the Divine Mother's power and love to flow through your life. You may have lived a long time wondering why things aren't working out and questioning whether or not you deserve abundance. The answer to your question is: You absolutely do deserve to live a life full of abundance, bliss, and so much more. You deserve certainty. You deserve the guidance you can depend on, especially when it appears the ground continues to shake and shift beneath your feet.

You deserve the peace of mind that comes with allowing Divine Feminine energy to lead the way and show you a better path to reach your desires. You'll discover how beautiful life can be when you find the sweet spot between the Divine Masculine and the Divine Feminine, channeling in equal portions easily and gracefully.

It is time to stop repressing that which is natural; grace, abundance, peace, prosperity, vitality, and life are your birthright. These and more are qualities that the toxic masculinity of the patriarchy has continued to suppress through heavy-handed methods, like war, violence, deliberate starvation, the calculated continuance of poverty, and the insidious nature of slavery – which is still alive and practiced today.

Unlike other books on the topic, this one is written in simple English, making it easy to understand. Every concept is clearly explained, leaving no room for confusion. The ideas build upon one another sequentially, allowing you to grasp precisely what you need to learn and how to apply your newfound knowledge. You'll appreciate the clarity and practicality of the instructions on these pages. So, if you are ready to discover the power of the Divine Feminine in your life, there's no reason to dilly-dally! Head on to the first chapter.

Chapter 1: What Is the Divine Feminine?

Take a good look at society, and you'll notice an abundance of masculine energy. It doesn't matter what you look at, whether politics, religion, business, or other spheres of life. You'll see the shadow side of masculinity holding swaying human affairs. Now, there's nothing wrong with masculinity or the Divine Masculine energy. However, you need to balance the masculine and feminine energies within you to live a full life. Thankfully, people are becoming more aware of this truth and seeking more information about the Divine Feminine. This energy is awakening within you, and that's why you've chosen this book.

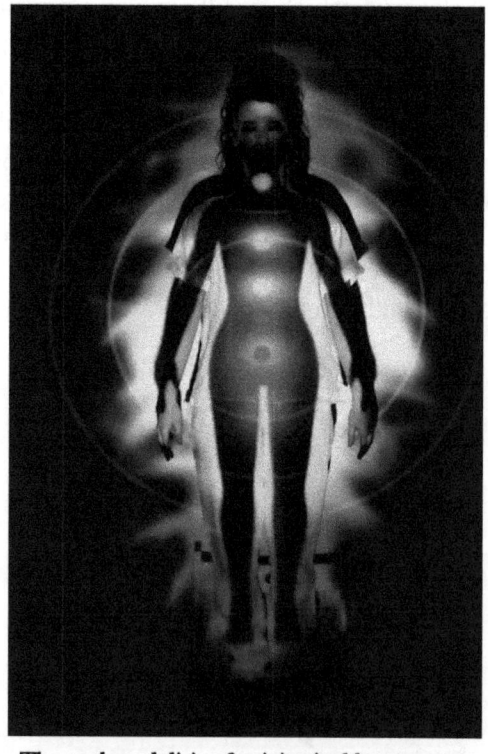

The awakened divine feminine is able to connect with several aspects of her spiritual self.[1]

Before anything else, it's essential to define the Divine Feminine so there are no misunderstandings. The definition is an absolute necessity, especially in light of the present times, with many demonizing anything masculine without understanding that both energies are required in balance.

The Divine Feminine

Everything in life has the Divine Masculine and the Divine Feminine energy within. The same can be said of you. Like many others, you have made do with living in your masculine energy, but it's becoming apparent something's missing from living this way. Through spiritual breadcrumbs, you have been led to this point to discover the true meaning of the Divine Feminine, why this energy is essential, and how you can integrate it into your life to bring balance, ease, and flow to your every waking moment.

The Divine Feminine is a force that has existed since before the dawn of time. It is one half of a whole that is necessary for the creation of all life, known and unknown, still playing a major part in the universe's sustenance. You can think of this energy as the soil. Regardless of what you plant in it, it does not discriminate and will sustain the life of that seed, allowing it to blossom and grow to its fullest potential and continue to nourish it beyond this point. And it's impossible to separate yourself from this energy. Sure, you may not have allowed yourself to flow with it, but it has always been with you.

You can't have the Divine Masculine without the Divine Feminine and vice versa. It has nothing to do with your gender. These energies do not care about how you identify. You may be a man or a woman or identify as something else; still, you have both energies within. When the Divine Masculine is the dominant energy in your life, you come from a place of excess action. You'll have a need to dominate others and exhibit aggressiveness in everything you do and say. You can't understand there are other ways to accomplish your goals that do not require the willingness to cut down others relentlessly. On the flip side, when the Divine Feminine is overly relied upon, you won't make much progress. You lose your power and don't know where to draw the line with yourself or with others. You look at your life, and you get the sense that nothing is moving or changing.

Humans are instinctively drawn toward change and progress. So, when the Divine Feminine does not have the Divine Masculine balancing it out in your life, you feel stuck. The world is one of duality, born from the ultimate reality of unity. The manifestation of the universe is a combination of goddess and god, showing up as woman and man, yang and yin — all of which embody the ultimate forces of the Divine Feminine and the Divine Masculine.

The Qualities of the Divine Feminine

You now recognize the importance of allowing the Divine Feminine energy to flow into and through your life. But how can you tell when you're giving the Divine Mother free rein in your life? These are the qualities of her energy.

- **Intuition.** Split the word into two, and you have "in" and "tuition," teaching that comes from within. It is the knowledge you receive through "illogical" or "irrational" means. It's about knowing things without understanding how. Your intuition is your gut feeling, which, if you follow, leads you to the best results. It warns and keeps you safe from danger or directs you to something you've always desired. Your intuition tells you who's a good person and who isn't. You don't have to wait for them to do something before you know for sure who someone is — not if you follow your intuition's guidance. Choosing to trust your intuition over everything else makes it stronger. Some people have worked on their intuition to the point where they can predict what will happen in the future.

  The more you embody the Divine Feminine, the more intuitive you are. It doesn't matter if you are a woman or a man, as the moment you accept the Divine Feminine influence in your life by embodying it, the more powerful this quality will be. It's no accident that historically, women have always been more intuitive than men. It doesn't mean that men cannot become intuitive. So, if you're a man reading this, know that you, too, can develop your intuition; *don't feel excluded!*

- **Creativity.** The creative process is a feminine one. The most basic form of creativity is childbirth, which only women are naturally equipped to do. Of course, it's impossible to conceive a child without a man playing his part, but childbirth is the woman's ability, seeing as she has a womb in which the child is nurtured before being released into the world when due. Now, what about creativity in every other aspect of life? For some reason, when many think about creativity, they only think about creating movies and cartoons, writing books, singing, acting, dancing, crafts, etc. However, creativity is in every aspect of life. You could be an accountant, but your process still requires creativity.

Using creativity correctly, you can elevate your financial status. Embody the Divine Feminine energy to experience more of its beautiful influence in your life.

You have an energetic body that is made up of energy centers called *chakras*. By unblocking your sacral chakra, you'll experience more creativity in every aspect of your life. This energy center allows the Divine Feminine energy to permeate your existence, and interestingly, it is also the seat of sexual energy required for giving life. There is a connection between sexuality and creativity, both of which are necessary for self-expression. Those who have allowed the Divine Feminine to be more prominent in their lives have no problem with self-expression. They are typically some of the most creative people you'll meet because it is impossible to create without being connected to your intuition and living a life where your heart (rather than your head) drives your choices.

- **Empathy.** The Divine Feminine energy is the fuel for empathy. This basic human trait is much more pronounced in people with the Divine Feminine flowing unimpeded in their lives. Activating or remaining in the Divine Feminine's energy is impossible without being empathetic.

Empathy allows you to connect with your intuition and become a better communicator. Some people think empathy is simply the ability to logically understand what someone else is experiencing. However, it's much more than that. It's about slipping into someone else's shoes and looking at things through their eyes so you genuinely feel their feelings. You embody the sorrow, hurt, anger, joy, ecstasy, or whatever else is in the other's heart.

By deliberately considering what someone else may be going through and how they feel, you encourage the flow of the Divine Feminine. You connect with it better. You find it's not worth judging others because judgment causes toxicity in the connections you share with the people in your life. It's so easy to assume you'd do things differently if you were in the other person's shoes, but the truth is, there's no way to tell whether you would have made different choices in their position.

- **Compassion.** Once you've developed empathy, the next step is to build compassion. These qualities are connected. How? There's no way you could possibly be compassionate if you don't have empathy. Compassion is positive. It causes you to act to alleviate the pain and suffering of those you feel an empathic connection to. The Divine Feminine energy is the urge that drives you toward compassionate actions and choices.

- **Balance.** Where it's more typical of masculine energy to push things to the extreme, the Divine Feminine calls for *balance*. Balance is required in every aspect of your life, whether it's work, love, money, health, etc. Balancing something means finding the sweet spot between two extremes rather than pushing toward one end or the other. It's learning to love others without losing yourself in the process and forgetting you should show yourself love, too. It's being wise about spending your money but not being so frugal that you don't enjoy yourself. It's doing all you can to care for your health by working out, eating right, and getting enough rest without being so extreme that you can't attend to other aspects of your life. It's giving your very best regarding your work, but not so much that you lose yourself, and work becomes your entire identity.

If you observe Mother Nature, you'll realize that balance is in everything. When it rises, the sun doesn't remain pinned to a spot in the sky. It must also *set*. It shines, but not forever, since rain and snow must fall. There is hot and cold, left and right, up and down. The duality of life does not mean you should align yourself with one extreme. The truth about extremes is that they are different sides of the same coin. With the Divine Feminine energy, you'll understand this profoundly and notice your life is balanced as a result.

The Ancient Roots of the Divine Feminine

The Divine Feminine isn't a new concept. Even before there was a term for this energy, it always has been. It's primordial. Comb through history, and you'll find that it's always been honored in some way, as humans realized long ago the sacredness and influence of this force. Even in ancient times, people were aware of the power responsible for creation and fertility, and they represented it using the image of the Great Mother Goddess. Many societies and religions from past epochs highly regarded the Great Mother. Before there was a change in philosophy, this was the norm. The patriarchal religions elbowed their way to the forefront of human consciousness. These religions and philosophies used such brute force in their takeover that they successfully made the Divine Feminine a forgotten concept.

Before the masculine took over, priestesses were more prominent in religious affairs, rituals, etc. Women were revered as the bastions of excellence in the spiritual realm of life's affairs, and there was unmistakable peace in society, unparalleled by whatever has been the most peaceful culture or time under the patriarchy's rule. Things remained blissful until warrior societies slowly but surely grew. Examine ancient societies, religions, and cultures, and you'll find they honored the Mother archetype in the form of Mother Earth, depicting her in various art forms and telling stories and myths about her. That's a far cry from today's reality, with the prominent three religions — Islam, Judaism, and Christianity — being centered on the worship of a masculine God.

Gaia

The ancestors thought of the Earth as the Divine Feminine in physical form, seeing it as a female being that continues to give and sustain life. The way they saw it, the Earth gives life by nurturing plants, which animals depend on. Predators may feast on prey fed by plants. Your ancestors understood that the Mother alone was responsible for the relentless flow of life and that when plants and animals die, they return to her only to be born again. In other words, the Divine Feminine is about the cycle of birth, death, and rebirth. There would be no ecosystem without Mother Earth. She is the ultimate life-giver, nurturer, and healer. Creation and destruction are in her hands, both essential to life's continuation. But where, precisely, was the idea of the Earth as a mother first documented? The first reference to this idea is in the writings of the ancient Greeks, who referred to the Divine Feminine as Gaia, the mother of creation and the Earth goddess, in the 7th century BCE. According to the Greeks, all life began with only three Divine beings: Chaos, Gaia, and Eros, with Gaia being the mother of every Divine being.

Venus of Willendorf

Head over to Austria, and you'll find one of the oldest representations of the Divine Feminine in Willendorf, Venus of Willendorf. Historians believe she was crafted between 25,000 and 20,000 BCE, back in the Paleolithic epoch. The sculpture may be small, being only 4.3 inches in height, but her significance to the people stands immeasurably far above and beyond that height! The figure has no face. She has an overhanging stomach, acting as a roof over her prominent pubic region. Above her belly are large breasts. Together, these features represent life, pregnancy, birth, and fertility. This sculpture is faceless to shift the focus to her body, which signifies everything about life and the sustenance thereof. Interestingly, there aren't as many masculine figurines from the Paleolithic times as there are feminine ones, clarifying that the society of the time was matriarchal.

Sculpture of Venus of Willendorf, one of the oldest representations of the Divine Feminine.[2]

The Sleeping Lady of Malta

The Sleeping Lady of Malta.[3]

The Sleeping Lady is another illustration of the Divine Mother in a Neolithic burial ground in Malta. Its precise location is the Gal Saflieni Hypogeum, now a UNESCO World Heritage Site. She's depicted as a woman with curves, fast asleep on a bed, lying on her side. Historians and scholars believe she's connected with the eternal sleep of death because the figure was discovered at a burial site. She was seen as the Goddess of Regeneration, reigning supreme over the processes of birth, death, and rebirth. It's also hypothesized that she was revered at a time when people were transitioning from hunting and gathering to farming, cultivating their crops, enabling them to remain in one spot rather than live a nomadic life. This switch in lifestyle came with its attendant issues, which would've put an end to their livelihood if they hadn't addressed it. So, it was natural that they turned toward the Divine Feminine, who they knew could help them with cultivation and procreation.

The Cycladic Female Figurines

The Cycladic female depiction of the Divine Mother differs from the previously mentioned goddesses, as she isn't voluptuous. Looking at her belly, you can see a gentle swell indicating pregnancy. This figure has her hands folded beneath her breasts, a pose reminiscent of other images from Cyprus, Palestine, Syria, and other Eastern Mediterranean regions. In those times, people died much more often and younger than presently. Because of this high mortality rate, the people sought the favor of the Mother Goddess through these statuettes, asking her to protect and keep them safe.

The Cycladic female figurine.'

The Snake Goddess of Crete

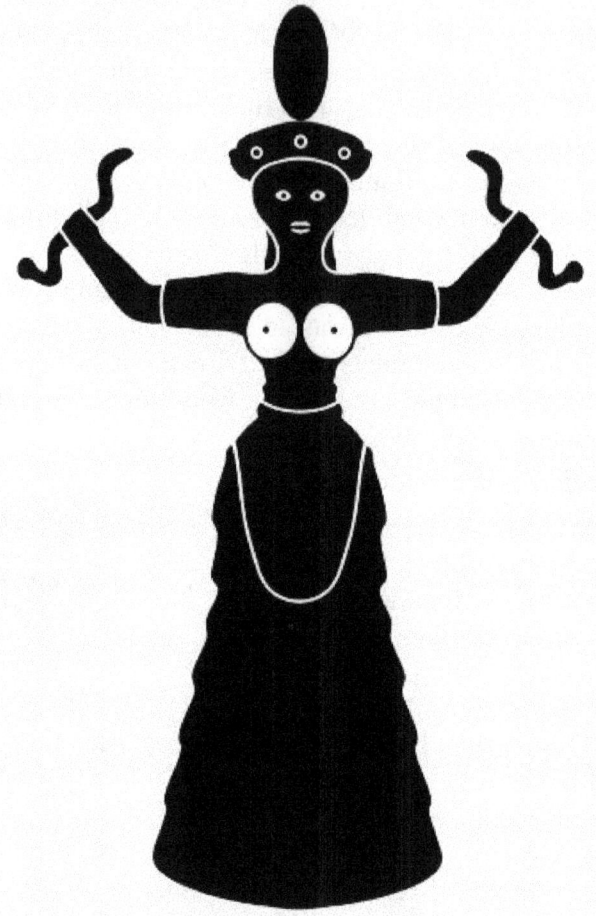

The Snake Goddess of Crete.[5]

    The Snake Goddess from the Knossos palace is from circa 1600 BCE. This portrayal of the Goddess was revered by the people of Crete, specifically those in the ancient Minoan Civilization. She's different from the previous iterations of Mother God because her design is much more intricate. Her sensuality is undeniable, as she's dressed in a fancy skirt with her breasts bare, both symbolizing the nourishment of breast milk, fertility, and the sexuality of the feminine. She has a snake in each hand, and for good reason, since snakes are connected to the underworld, regeneration, and healing. The Minoans held women in high regard in societal and religious matters, and their life was built on an impressively organized system where agriculture was efficiently handled.

Maat

Maat was the embodiment of justice, balance, and truth.[6]

Ancient Egyptians had a plethora of female goddesses. These expressions of the Divine Feminine were the bastions of order, morality, conception, fertility, values, etc. Maat was about maintaining the harmony of the cosmos. She was the embodiment of justice, balance, and truth. Maat's followers believed that when they passed on, the weight of their hearts would be measured against that of the ostrich feather she wore on her head. Those whose hearts were as light as Maat's feather could pass over to paradise, ruled by Osiris.

Why Should You Connect with the Divine Feminine?

You don't need to subscribe to certain religious beliefs to benefit from the Divine Feminine energy flowing into your life. It is helpful to know because you can begin to transform your life right now. You should want the touch of the Divine Mother in your life for the following reasons:

1. You'll experience increased intuition, which will steer you where you want to go and away from danger or anything that doesn't serve you.
2. You'll become a more compassionate person, which opens you up to experiencing compassion and care from others, too.
3. You'll learn to relax and trust life more. It's a necessary gift in a world designed to give you more reasons to be anxious and insecure each day. The Divine Feminine will teach you how to relax and receive and manifest your dreams by energetically aligning with your desires rather than using brute force.
4. You'll be more in tune with life, which will help your creativity.
5. Your awareness and allowance of Divine Feminine energy will lead you to find a balance between the feminine and the masculine. As a result, you'll be in a much more powerful position than others, equipped to change your life as needed because you have the direct action of the Divine Masculine and the intuitive guidance and magnetism of the Divine Feminine.

By exploring and interacting with the Mother energy, you'll develop an intuitive comprehension of spiritual matters. Why does that matter? It's because everything in life comes from spirit, so if you can crack the code by finding the balance between both polarities, you'll have a life you love more and more each day.

Once more, nothing about the Divine Feminine or Divine Masculine has to do with gender, so it's best not to tie it to simplistic affairs, which are of no consequence in the ultimate reality of life. That would be reductive. Spirit isn't about those things. While many combat the idea of the Divine Feminine by arguing it's feminism wearing a new mask, they're absolutely incorrect. Also, the Divine Feminine isn't an excuse for people to push their borderline fanatical ideologies whether or not multiple genders or "being non-binary" is valid — *never mind that "non-binary" automatically creates a binary!*

Some people have attempted to weaponize the Divine Feminine by labeling it an attack on their religion or an attempt to encourage a female answer to the red pill movement that's just as toxic. Once more, the Divine Feminine and Divine Masculine are not about these spiritually immature debates. Knowledge of this energy has to be spread to allow the integration of both halves, which exist in every person and everything. This integration will create the possibility for a much more harmonious life than what humans have had to contend with in recent history.

If everyone were to learn to find the balance between these divine polarities, they would quickly realize how moot certain debates and conversations are. Humans are much more than their sexualities, genders, or how they identify. You, too, will be empowered by understanding the truth about the Divine Feminine. You can connect with the Goddess within and see for yourself how your life changes exponentially for the better.

Prompts to Connect with the Divine Feminine

1. Can you recall a moment in life or a dream where you felt the nature of the Divine Feminine energy powerfully, expressed through creativity, intuition, nurturing, or any other of its qualities?
2. Based on the qualities of the Divine Feminine explained earlier in this chapter, could you think of three ways to promote the flow of the Divine Feminine energy each day?

Chapter 2: Exploring the Divine Feminine Archetypes

Before exploring the different Divine Feminine archetypes, you need a proper understanding of what archetypes are. Swiss psychiatrist Carl Jung is the brilliant mind who developed the concept of archetypes in the 20th century. But that doesn't mean these archetypes didn't exist before he identified and named them. They are intended to show you that femininity has multiple facets. Archetypes are patterns of behavior and expression that exist in everyone.

The female archetypes are the embodiments of various characteristics and experiences that are unique to femininity. Does this imply there are only as many kinds of women as there are feminine archetypes?

No.

Femininity has multiple facets.[7]

For one thing, the female archetypes apply to everyone, female and male. For another, the idea of archetypes isn't meant to put people into neatly labeled boxes but to offer various perspectives on how feminine qualities are embodied and expressed.

Are these archetypes only negative or positive? They have their light and shadow aspects. Life is complex, and so are people. It's unrealistic to think that any idea, thing, or person is all light or all darkness, all good or all bad. This black-and-white thinking only serves to inhibit true understanding of spirituality and, by extension, life. Another thing to keep in mind as you delve into archetypes is that they're not death sentences, static and unchanging.

It is possible to experience different archetypes at the same time or to switch from one to another. Your archetype may depend on what phase of life you're in. Also, you may change archetypes, embodying one at home and a different one at work and yet another regarding health, finances, etc.

With your understanding of feminine archetypes, you'll know what drives you, how you handle your relationships, and what choices you'll likely settle on. You'll understand how you navigate life and why others respond to you as they do.

The Four Main Feminine Archetypes

The main female archetypes are the **Maiden, Mother, Wild Woman, and Crone**. You can think of them as spiritual or energetic blueprints you can plug into. It's best to honor each of these in your life because you'll fail if you choose to suppress them. Even worse, you'll call forth the dark aspect of this archetype in your life, the shadow side. The result? You'll experience psychological problems like depression and anxiety, with your life feeling wildly out of balance. Your relationships and physical health will break down as you attempt to suppress these aspects of yourself. Therefore, you have to know them and learn to love them.

1. The Maiden

Light Aspects: Openness, potential, innocence, adaptability, new beginnings, purity, playfulness, receptivity, and curiosity.

Shadow Aspects: A refusal to release childhood indecisiveness, self-doubt, resistance to growth, fear, escapism, stagnation, naivety.

Spiritual Correspondences: Intuition, water, springtime, the moon, new beginnings, sunrise.

Goddesses: Osun, Aset, Asase Yaa, Hestia, Artemis, Amaterasu, Guanyin, Rhiannon.

The maiden.[8]

About This Archetype: The Maiden is the embodiment of purity. The common misconception is that "maidenhood" in this context refers to sexuality, but really, it's a state of mind. It's about a state of autonomy and independence, where you refuse to allow anyone or anything a pedestal in your life. You're your own person. The energy of the Maiden is strong, dynamic, full of youth and joie de vivre. When you allow this energy to flow, you're magnetic to the good things in life. You're full of positivity, keeping your mind and heart open to the new, unafraid of throwing yourself wholeheartedly into unfamiliar realms, excitedly asking, "What if?"

The Maiden has no responsibilities weighing her down and no negativity or doubt from past experiences. When you embody this energy, you're assertive, unafraid to plan, and willing to connect with others as you're at your most sociable. You know there's much to discover about yourself and life, and you embrace every chance to learn. You take care of yourself, taking the time to dress well and strengthen your body through exercise.

2. The Mother

Light Aspects: Protection, fertility, creativity, care, compassion, selflessness, nurturing, empathy, and abundance.

Shadow Aspects: Smothering, martyrdom, sacrifice, control, neglect of self, resistance to change, overprotectiveness, and a desperate clinging to the past.

Spiritual Correspondences: Summer, stability, full moon, groundedness, Earth.

Goddesses: Isis, Kali, Demeter (Ceres), Gaia, Terra Mater, Cybele, Maia, Nammu.

The mother.⁹

About This Archetype: The Mother archetype is the embodiment of fertility. She is sensuous in all her ways, never lacking for anything since she is abundance itself. As the Mother, your compassion knows no bounds, and neither does your generosity. You're also at your most creative, supportive, caring, and nurturing. The Mother isn't one to spoil senselessly, as her love is sweet, soft, yet tough. Across religions, cultures, and myths, the Mother is the Earth herself. She is the one true body upon which the flora and fauna of life "live and move and have their being."

When you express your inner Mother, you slow down and focus on being present, understanding that the here and now is the ultimate gift life offers. You're full of gratitude for where you are and willing to share this with the people you appreciate in your life. Even your clothing reflects this energy, as you favor more comfortable clothing that doesn't hug too tightly or restrict your movement. If you want to amplify this energy more, you'd be hard-pressed to find a better way than spending time in nature. As the Mother, you care for yourself, shelving everything you allow to become more important than living and realizing there's no business or job more important than living and being human. You get in touch with your heart, only doing what feels right as you realize it's the only obligation you have.

3. The Wild Woman

Light Aspects: Transformation, potential, courage, freedom, resilience, wisdom, self-expression, passion, creativity.

Shadow Aspects: Volatile emotions, aggression, jealousy, self-sabotage, recklessness, possessiveness of fear of commitment, destructiveness.

Spiritual Correspondences: Fire, energy, passion, autumn, wild places, the solar plexus, the South.

Goddesses: Sekhmet, Bastet, Kali, Diana, Lilith, Frey, the Morrigan.

The wild woman.[10]

About This Archetype: The Wild Woman archetype is darker than the previous two, and for some reason, many misunderstand this archetype. They don't realize this archetype is a healer in her own right. Consider the image of a medicine woman, in touch with nature, knowing its secrets, and refusing to be tamed or "cultured." This archetype signifies the soul waking up to the true, ultimate reality of life after a long time of being fast asleep, lulled into a comatose state by the lies and illusions of physical life. She is the Wild Woman only because she defies logic, being greater than it, tapping into the realms of the magical, which society neither takes seriously nor makes room for.

Thanks to the Wild Woman, you have full access to your inner knowing, remaining permanently connected to your intuition. It's this archetype that carries healing power. There's nothing rational about her ways. She is a terror to those who cling desperately to the need to make sense of things. The human mind fears what it doesn't understand and cannot predict. The Wild Woman will remain unknown to the mind that hasn't accepted that there are things too great to be contained by the step-by-step sequence characteristic of logical, rational thought.

The patriarchal system of doing things has worked ceaselessly to erase everything about the Wild Woman, silencing those who dare to speak up about this archetype or express it. However, she's very present, and you can connect with her. The reason she is so suppressed isn't that she's problematic but because society's ills and restrictions would crumble were she allowed full expression, and some would hate for that to happen. You may have become a willing participant in her suppression, not allowing her to express herself in your life. The previous statement isn't to shame you but to help you break free from the sleepy spell cast on you through educational and media conditioning.

You need to step back from connecting with others and withdraw within to embody the Wild Woman. Also, you shouldn't give your power or attention away to screens. Instead, connect with yourself through mindful practices like meditation. The Wild Woman has boundaries she fiercely protects, saying no to anything she doesn't want without remorse. She enjoys nature, expresses her rage, and doesn't shy away from shadow work to reveal her darker aspects and integrate them.

4. The Crone

Light Aspects: Acceptance, death and rebirth, mystery, release, insight, transformation, guidance, and wisdom.

Shadow Aspects: Isolation, cynicism, an excessive desire to control, a desperate clinging to the past, cynicism, bitterness, fear of death, and a deep resistance to change.

Spiritual Correspondences: Winter, twilight, dark moon, endings and beginnings, the void.

Goddesses: Cailleach, Baba Yaga, Cybele, Hecate, and Las Cacareas (The Old Cacklers).

The crone.[11]

About This Archetype: She's known as the Wise Woman and isn't accorded the respect she deserves. People only think of this archetype as old, infertile, and inactive. They think of her as the loss of beauty, but that's not what this archetype is about. In popular culture, she is shown as a wicked witch, an old woman cast out from society, banished to the furthermost reaches of the community. She's described as bitter with a chip on her shoulder, willing to destroy with trickery.

However, there's a power to her that many are unaware of. Her slowness embodies mystery, which stands in contrast to the fast-paced life many are used to. Her life is rich and full of wisdom and meaning. She is in a position where she isn't required to achieve anything, nor does the allure of "productivity" seduce her. She is free from all expectations, putting her in the singular position of having nothing to lose. That is the actual reason she's villainized. The person with nothing to lose has true freedom, and it is a power that can bring even the greatest to their knees.

The Other Feminine Archetypes

The Warrior

The Warrior archetype is about justice. She's not afraid to fight. When you embody this archetype, you find it difficult to condone wrongdoing, say nothing, and act like it didn't happen. You're not a person who will mince words. You're unafraid to tell it exactly as it is. You do more than speak up; you act to correct injustice when you can. Whenever you cannot help others, you'll rally every resource and person you can to assist you.

As the Warrior, you don't care about your personal safety because you are committed to the mission of setting things right. Think of yourself as a mother bear, fiercely protecting her young to death. That's what it means to embody this archetype. You couldn't care less about whether or not you make enemies as long as you restore justice and balance. You aren't concerned about being inconvenienced or having your comfort taken from you as long as you ensure justice prevails.

Being a Warrior means you are a physical person. Your mind and body possess stamina, strength, and resilience beyond compare. You're an inspiration to others around you. You know how to transmute the energies of rage and anger and channel them toward productive ends. Women in history who have embodied this archetype include Rosa Parks and Joan of Arc.

The Enchantress

The Enchantress archetype is about mystery. Her function is seduction. In this energy, you are more open to the unknown, daring to leave your comfort zone for the wild world beyond what you understand. As the Enchantress, you are no longer tethered to your past because you refuse to be defined by it. Instead, you are magnetized toward the future, drawn by the siren call of your dreams and the possibility of what could be. The Enchantress's aura is magnetic, drawing everyone in. She sweetly helps you realize your truest desires and dares you to pursue them. Why? She wants you to see how much more magical your life could become if you left the comfort of the familiar.

Jacqueline Kennedy is a historical enchantress.[12]

The Enchantress is charismatic, and barely a soul can withstand her charm. You are confident when you embody this archetype, and it's hard not to see that. You're a bold, brilliant light, so bright that you force others to do a double-take whenever you walk into the room. The world is your stage. You are the leading lady; everyone else is a supporting actor or extra — but you are not an obnoxious leading lady! You're a mirror for others, showing them how much more they could be. Those who are too insecure to withstand the brightness of your light have no choice but to turn away or get out of your way because you have no intention of dimming your glory for their comfort. Historical enchantresses include Mata Hari, Cleopatra, Eva Peron, Jacqueline Kennedy, and Madame de Pompadour.

The Lover

Playing out this archetype makes you passionate and on fire for life. A sensual person, nothing escapes your notice. You pick up on everything from textures to smells, colors to sounds, etc. You're a person who understands the value of being present, ever rooted in the here and now. You realize that life is romance — not in the shallow way depicted in books and movies, but in how you approach everything with a lover's heart.

As present as you are, you recognize that the past has valuable treasures. When life becomes too dark and burdens too heavy to bear, you look for the good in your situation. The love you carry in your heart that helps you relentlessly press forward, unafraid and willing to drop your ego with reckless abandon. As the Lover, you're aware of your worth. You know that you have unquestionable value. Therefore, nothing is too good for you.

You recognize that you deserve the best in life and understand that others do, too. No one is more aware of the fleeting nature of life than you are, so you savor every sweet drop of life's nectar and offer yourself in full in return. You're aware that your love puts you in a vulnerable position where you could be hurt, but you understand it's par for the course. It's not enough to make you withdraw or retreat. If you'd like to understand this archetype better, you should read Rumi's works.

The Healer

The Healer archetype considers everything to be whole. Others may see brokenness and imperfection, but that's not how she views the world. Her heart is sensitive and bleeds for others, unable to look upon people who are suffering without feeling empathy and compassion. Similar to the Warrior archetype, the Healer archetype does not rest in the face of pain and suffering. However, her approach is gentler.

When you are the Healer, you take care of others *and yourself* because you understand that you cannot give what you don't have. You know the intricate connection between body, mind, and spirit and that all three aspects of self must be nurtured and tended to. The Healer naturally knows what would help every situation. The body and the Earth have wisdom beyond compare, and as the Healer, you have the intuitive ability to connect with this wisdom. So, you know what would work as a solution or a healing medicine at any point in time, regardless of the ailment. You will embody this energy more with a mindfulness practice like meditation. Mother Teresa would have been a great example of the Healer archetype, but she gave in to her dark side and expressed it toxically.

The Visionary

The Visionary is also called the *Prophet* or the *Seer*. Traditionally, the people who embody this archetype are known for predicting the future. There's more to this archetype than envisioning possibilities. She takes action, channeling her energy toward inspiring herself and others to move toward what could be. One of the most fascinating things about The Visionary is the power that lies within her voice. She has a way with words that draws hearts and minds toward her message. She understands the power of the spoken word and how it can move people toward healing or destruction.

Many people fear the unknown, refusing to try something new because it's never been done before. However, this archetype couldn't care less about whether or not a thing has ever been done. She's far more interested in potential, which lies beyond the realms of the familiar and the known. She transmutes the energy of fear into courage and faith. With these traits, she rides into new territories and conquers them for the benefit of everyone. Famous oracles include Cassandra of Troy, Deborah the Prophet, Miriam (Moses's sister), and the Delphi Oracle Sybil.

The Creator

The Creator desires to express life and beauty in every way possible. She can craft worlds yet unimagined by any mind and bring them to pass. Where others see what eyes will allow them to see, the Creator sees beyond what is. Not only that, but she can also bring what she sees into physical reality. If you embody the Creator archetype, you understand you're not doing the creation yourself. Instead, you're serving as a channel or a conduit to allow creativity to flow through you and take whatever form it will, whether it's a pair of socks you're knitting or a piece of music you're composing. The Creator is most fulfilled when she can create. If you've been feeling depressed or out of touch with life, you may find it helpful to tap into this side of yourself. Excellent examples of this archetype include Jane Austen, Virginia Woolf, Augusta Savage, Louise Bourgeois, and Sapho.

An example of the creator archetype is Virginia Woolf.[18]

The Queen

This archetype is all about building a legacy. Every archetype is capable of being a leader. However, the Queen is a natural at this. You should know that of all the archetypes, she is the most masculine-leaning. When you are the embodiment of the Queen, you understand how powerful it is to approach every problem using strategy, and you realize that your goal is to serve a purpose higher than your personal ambitions. Your decisions aren't selfish, as you settle upon them only after thorough consideration of everyone and everything that will be affected. You realize the importance of considering the consequences. While you recognize the allure of living life on your own terms, you choose to sacrifice it in pursuit of goals beyond the ordinary. By doing this, you plunge your life into meaningful depths far beyond what others could possibly fathom.

Like the Warrior, you have unparalleled energy. You don't allow anything to take your focus away from your highest calling and purpose. While you're always paying attention to various perspectives and opinions on what would be the best course of action, you alone are the final arbiter who determines what should happen. When you make your pronouncements, they're not up for negotiation or discussion. Everyone must fall in line with your decree. Individuals who exhibited the true Queen energy include Margaret Thatcher, Queen Elizabeth I, Queen Elizabeth II, and Queen Victoria; Athena, the Greek goddess of martial strategy and wisdom; Pharaoh Hapshetsut; and Pharaoh Nefertiti.

The Priestess

Nothing matters more to the Priestess archetype than enlightenment. Being a mystic, she desires to see the connection between all things physical and spiritual. As a priestess, you do not condemn anything as being profane because you realize that all things spring from one source and, therefore, are sacred. You have the critical role of reminding people of their divine origins and calling them back to their true selves. As the Healer and Warrior do, you desire nothing more than to bring things back to their proper order. However, you fight this battle on the spiritual, energetic plane.

You bring people back to the truth of who they are by transmuting darkness into light. You've spent time in isolation, studying the ways of spirit and how it expresses itself in the physical world. Intuitively aware of the old ways and knowing how to use them, you create a life that works for all. Others may think of miracles as one-offs, things that only happen now and then. But for you, miracles are moment-to-moment things. Where people see nothing but a dead end, you see a way through every time.

You know you could never be stuck because you're never alone. You carry within the divine power of the ultimate source of all things. This is the power of God. You recognize that even though things seem random and chaotic, they are according to a divine script that cannot be altered and ultimately leads to the enlightenment of everyone. You take the verse, "Ask, and you shall be given; seek, and you shall find; knock, and it shall be opened unto you," quite literally — not because you're delusional, but because that has been your life experience. Examples of people who have embodied this energy include Rabiah al-Adawiyya al-Qaysyya, Lalleshwari, Hildegard of Bingen, Therese of Lisieux, Mirabai, Alexandra David-Neel, and Hazrat Babajan.

What's Your Archetype?

Having read through all these archetypes, you may find yourself a bit confused because you recognize yourself in each one. It almost makes you assume that the whole concept of archetypes must be nonsense, doesn't it? There's no such thing as having one particular archetype. You can fluidly move from one to another or embody several at the same time. However, you may have noticed that you approach life through the lens of a specific archetype more than the others.

This awareness will help you navigate your existence much better than you've been doing. Why? You'll find a way to balance all these archetypes, moving fluidly from one to another as needed, because every situation in life requires different strategies and tactics to approach them. When you can recognize your dominant feminine archetypes and integrate them, you transform your life for the better. Before heading on to the next chapter, here are questions to reflect on to understand your inner world better:

1. Of all the archetypes presented, which feels closest to your aspirations and experiences?
2. As you ponder individual aspects of your life (spiritual, mental, physical, and emotional), which archetypes do you embody the most in each one?
3. Which archetype were you the least connected to? Why do you think that is?
4. Which archetypes do you wish you could embody but feel like you can't? Why?

The chapters to come will help you discover who you are and connect you to your unique expressions of the Divine Feminine energy, particularly regarding the four major feminine archetypes.

Chapter 3: Discovering the Inner Goddess

Your inner goddess is nothing like the mask you've had to put on to get through daily life. Her authentic self resides within you, and her power and confidence are beyond compare. She doesn't care about what society expects from you, and she has neither the time nor the patience for self-doubt. You honor your true self when you allow her to manifest in your life. Your strengths shine through, and you no longer hide your passions

Unleash the goddess within.[14]

for fear of being put down or mocked. You don't care because you know there's nothing more fulfilling than being your true self. She is that part of you that helps you be inspired to create and will encourage you through the darkest and worst of times.

The Benefits of Connecting with Your Inner Goddess

Everyone wants to experience personal growth and be their best, but not everyone knows how. Well, there's no better way to accomplish this goal than by getting in touch with the Divine goddess within you. As you do, you'll exhibit wisdom, power, and grace in all that you do, as you're no longer pulled this way or that by voices and circumstances around you. The goddess's tuition within leads you. There's nothing better because she knows what you need to thrive better than anyone else, and relying on her guidance will give you confidence in yourself.

Have you felt disconnected from life? Do you get the sense that you're not living out your purpose? Do you feel like your life has no direction? If so, you'll find many benefits from getting in touch with your inner goddess. As you do, you'll finally be able to look at everything in your life with acceptance.

Even the things you once criticized yourself terribly for will take on a new sheen, and you'll see there's not one part of who you are that doesn't deserve your love. You'll find how all your traits come together to make you who you are, someone irreplaceable. Every archetype has its light and dark side, and so does every human. When you accept this truth, you accept yourself, and you stop laboring under the burden of unfair comparisons. You put away the childish business of setting unrealistic expectations for yourself, and as a result, your self-esteem will be restored.

Another benefit of embracing your inner Goddess is you'll drop all the masks and costumes you've worn your entire life. You picked them up only as a matter of survival because you'd learned from an early point in life that the world wouldn't accept you if you showed up as your true self. However, these costumes and masks have done nothing more than dim your light. They've made you forfeit the radiance of your true, authentic self, shunning it and choosing the tattered rags of compliance and society's definition of acceptance, which, at its core, is fake. Society's acceptance is a message to your soul that you will be welcomed with open arms as long as you show up as anyone but who you are. That's not acceptance. That's a proposition forcing you to reject yourself, and it's so insidious because you remain unaware that no one has the power to reject you but you.

None of this is your fault, so don't waste time wallowing in self-blame. Now that you're aware of how the wool has been pulled over your eyes, you can fix the problem with the help of the Divine Goddess within you. Her light will cut through the darkness of inauthenticity if you allow it, and you'll remember how to breathe once more for the first time in a long time. You'll remember what makes you tick, what makes you smile, what fuels you with joy and life, and you'll go after these things with the relentless tenacity of a thousand shire horses, just as you did when you were a child before the world got into your head and told you who you were was unacceptable.

As you embody your authentic self, you draw a community of others close to you who share the same vision. You pull in people who have done away with the need to mask or pretend to be other than they are. As a result, your relationships will become sweeter, deeper, and fulfilling. You have the potential to embody the Divine Feminine in multiple facets, and when you do, you'll have no regrets for daring to take the plunge.

An Inclusive Guide to Identifying Who You Are: Maiden, Mother, Wild Woman, or Crone

Once more, you aren't excluded from channeling the Divine Feminine energy in your life by virtue of your gender. Regardless of how you identify, the odds are you are expressing one or a combination of the four main archetypes. But how do you determine which one you are? Use this guide to help you.

Begin by considering the things you value most in life. Your values will hint at the archetype you embody. If innocence matters to you more than anything else, then clearly, you are the Maiden. If you often find yourself taking on the role of a nurturer, you are the Mother. If you're in a phase of life when nothing matters to you more than your freedom, and you are relentlessly going after your passions, then the odds are you are the Wild Woman. What if you find that you're being more discerning as you make your choices and you've come to a place of genuine acceptance? Then, you're in touch with your inner Crone.

Look closely at where you currently are in life. In particular, what goals have you set for yourself? You embody the Maiden if you've decided to take on new adventures without reservations. You have her zest for life, untamed by disappointment. Is your desire to be a caring person? Are you building something, whether a family, relationships, or projects? Then, you are in your Mother energy. If you constantly throw yourself into the unexplored with reckless abandon, then you're being the Wild Woman. If you have to pause and reflect before taking action, seeking deeper meaning in your choices and your place in life, then you are in your Crone energy.

Examine your relationships with others in your life. As the Maiden, you're more likely to be curious and playful about connecting with new people and engaging with those you already know. As the Mother, you're the one people turn to whenever they need comfort, stability, and support. When you are the Wild Woman, while you enjoy your interactions with others, you are careful to ensure they do not dampen your passion, nor do you let them hinder your independence and freedom. As the Crone, you are the person in the friend group that everyone else turns to whenever they need advice to help them navigate difficult situations. You're the mentor. People in your life recognize your experience and wisdom, and they trust your guidance will be safe and sound.

Notice the activities and interests that give you pleasure and energy. Since the Maiden represents the start of life's cycle, she loves to learn new skills. If that's where you're at, then that's the energy you're embodying, and the only thing you're interested in is the growth that comes from learning. Do you find yourself drawn to activities where you play the role of the nurturer? Do you love helping people piece themselves together? Are you interested in bringing projects to completion? You're being the Mother.

As a Wild Woman, you refuse to be a part of anything that doesn't make your heart sing. Everything you're doing now brings you joy or is geared toward fulfilling your heart's desires. If you are more interested in activities that help you discover wisdom and apply the knowledge you've gathered practically, you're being the Crone. You're not in a hurry to get involved in things you don't care about.

Ask yourself what you're most afraid of and what your highest aspirations are. Are you terrified of never getting started on things that matter to you? Do you worry you'll never discover all life has to offer? You may be in your Maiden phase. If what scares you the most is the idea of having to let go or not controlling your life, then you may be exuding Mother energy. As a Wild Woman, nothing alarms you more than the thought of commitment because it means you'll lose your freedom and be tethered to one spot, which is the complete antithesis of this archetype's energy.

Next, consider your aspirations. The Maiden longs for growth. She knows there's so much more she could be. She realizes the only way to grow is to have experiences that are new to her. The Mother has done her exploring and now seeks more stability in her life, so if this is you, you're more interested in creating a rock-solid base for yourself. As the Wild Woman, you find that you are ready to be your truest, authentic self, which means becoming selfish — in a good way. You recognize it is time to give back to yourself. If you're the Crone, you desire to find inner peace and live a life that inspires all.

Practices for Integrating Your Dominant Feminine Archetype

For the Maiden:
1. Dedicate yourself to the practice of daily journaling. Why? As you journal, you discover more of who you are, which gives you a clue about what you should explore in your life. All you need is 15 minutes every day to enjoy the magical benefits of journaling. So, write about every new idea you have in your journal, what might have piqued your interest lately, how you plan to pursue said interest, and what you hope to accomplish for the day. Also, take five to 10 minutes at night to write in your journal, reflecting on how your day went and if it aligned with the goals you set for yourself at the start. Alternatively, you may prefer to use your night-time journaling to set your goals for the next day.
2. Make a list of everything that interests you and select what you'd like to make a hobby. You'll find the best things to pursue are completely brand new to you, as this will fuel your sense of wonder and your desire to explore the chosen subject further and your self-expression through that medium.
3. Think of one thing you could do to be kind to someone else every day. Ideally, they shouldn't be able to pay you back, and you shouldn't use your kindness as a bargaining chip either. You don't have to break the bank to be kind. A thoughtful compliment, a handwritten note of appreciation, or the willingness to volunteer your time and attention toward a cause or someone is an excellent place to start.

   Mantra: *"I satisfy my curiosity and embrace all possibilities."*

For the Mother:
1. Always keep your space clutter-free and organized, as this helps you feel in touch with your Mother energy. You'll benefit a lot by placing touches of nature around your home. Do you live with others? You'll benefit from having a special space decorated to your tastes, allowing you to return to embodying the Mother's vibe whenever you feel out of it.
2. You may find fulfillment in feeding others good, nutritious meals. Even if there's no one living with you, you can be Mother to yourself by taking care of nutritional needs, lovingly making them from scratch. When others are present, create a loving space of generosity and sharing by having everyone dine together in a grateful, mindful space.
3. Come up with ways you can be supportive of others around you, and see how you can show up for them as a mother would. You can do this in simple ways, like listening to someone with no judgment or observing the people in your life and offering them words or acts of service you know would make their lives easier to bear. Never miss the chance to demonstrate empathy. When you can't find an opportunity, you can always make one by being proactive and acting compassionately rather than waiting to be asked for help.

   Mantra: *"I nurture myself and others. I am safety, peace, warmth, and love."*

For the Wild Woman:
1. Consider activities that will center you in your body. The more you have to move, the better. So, try yoga, take up dancing, go for long hikes through nature, or if you're daring, try rock climbing, paragliding, etc.
2. Make a commitment to yourself never to speak anything that isn't the truth, and never apologize for saying things truthfully, as they are. Rather than suppress yourself, allow your creativity to run wild and free, and should it bump up against obstacles in the arbitrary norms society uses to dampen your spirit, go full throttle by leaning into being more of who you are without reservations.
3. Decide to be spontaneous. If you're invited somewhere, say yes, regardless of your plans (as long as it rings your bells, of course). Wholeheartedly embrace opportunities to abandon your comfort

zone. Never pause to think it through. Instead, trust that the magic of the Wild Woman will lead you to pleasant places and wonderful surprises.

Mantra: *"I feed my passion. I honor my freedom. I follow my heart with joy and abandon."*

For the Crone:
1. Prioritize silence. Make time each day to think about what you've learned or are learning, how you're faring, and where you're headed. Walking through nature or just sitting with it around you is excellent for these self-reflection sessions. You'll gain a lot from meditation. So, sit in silence for at least 10 to 15 minutes daily, allowing thoughts to come and go without latching on to or engaging them.
2. You should connect with mentors and the elders around you if you haven't already. They have much wisdom to share, and the more you talk with them, the more their knowledge will rub off on you. You'll discover you don't have to make mistakes when you can learn from the experiences of others who have already taken the paths you're considering. Don't just take and take without giving back when you're with them. Share what you've learned, too. Your interactions with these precious souls should be balanced, nurturing everyone.
3. Spend time contemplating that everything in life is powered by the mechanics of cycles. Nothing stays the same forever. In other words, you can ponder life and death, beginnings and endings, the times you should hold on versus the times you should release and let go of things. It helps you find inner peace and keeps you from spiraling into a negative thought vortex about the "evil" of endings. After all, every end is a new beginning worthy of acceptance and celebration.

Mantra: *"I accept life. I express wisdom. I'm at peace with endings and beginnings."*

How to Embrace and Transmute Your Shadow Traits

Regardless of the Divine Feminine archetype you're embodying, more often than not, you'll have shadow traits that overtake your light aspects.

How do you handle it when this happens? Here are some general tips:
1. Accept that these shadow traits are part and parcel of who you are. If you can't, they'll appear to hold you hostage. There's no way you'll learn what triggers you to express these dark aspects, let alone check them.
2. Become more self-aware by using meditation, contemplation, and journaling, among other similar practices, to get in touch with your authentic self. These tools will help you learn who you are, what you feel, what you think, and why you act the way you do. This is necessary before you can embrace your shadow side and transmute it.
3. Reframe your dark side by recognizing that it allows you to become the best version of yourself. If you are curious about it, you'll learn how it serves you, and you'll become a better person for it.
4. Pay attention to how you speak to yourself. If you're cruel and cutting, you need to cut that out right now and choose to be compassionate instead. If you wouldn't say it to a friend, you don't have permission to say it to yourself.

Here's specific advice for each of the 4 dominant Feminine archetypes.

For the Maiden: When your shadow side takes over, you're prone to being excessively dependent on others, acting irresponsibly, and being a little too naive for your own good. When you find yourself expressing these shadow traits, return to being curious. Become passionate about figuring things out for yourself. Curiosity will help you deal with your naivety, as you'll learn what you need to progress in life. If you're overwhelmed, don't be afraid to ask for help, but don't play the damsel in distress, either. You should always do your part to improve your situation. When you inevitably make mistakes (everyone does), be quick to take responsibility for your choices and turn your attention to seeking solutions.

For the Mother: As your shadow self, you tend to be overprotective. Naturally, this means you'll do what you think you must to keep the people you love safe. So, what's the problem here? Your overprotectiveness causes you to become manipulative. Eventually, when the people around you have had enough, they'll feel smothered by you. Therefore, your task is to learn to draw the line not just for others but for yourself. You can help so much, but no further. You must realize that people are autonomous beings who can and will make their own decisions, regardless of your advice or opinions.

So, practice trusting others and be deliberate about letting go when you sense you're being strong-handed or manipulative. Rather than be overprotective, recognize the independence of others and honor it. Rather than mentally strongarm someone into doing what you want through manipulation, communicate your concerns using reason and then get your hands off the wheel. Rather than smother people, give them the room to breathe and figure things out for themselves because this is the only way they'll grow.

For the Wild Woman: Wildness is fun, but when it gets out of hand, you can become a tad too reckless — some would argue, to the point of being destructive. You even sabotage yourself in the process. How can you combat this dark side? Learn to become more strategic in deciding what's worth the risk and what isn't. Take that wild, beautiful energy of yours and deliberately channel it only to constructive ends. The hallmarks of this archetype are adventure and spontaneity, two things that guarantee mistakes will be made. So, when you realize you've missed the mark, own your mistake. Recognize that accepting responsibility for things not going as you prefer isn't an indictment of who you are or your intrinsic value.

The transmutation work set out for you is to tame your recklessness unless and until you have enough information to unleash it however you please. Take your tendency to destroy and shift it toward creating, whether a project, a new skill, or connections with others. As for your self-sabotaging aspect, it can easily be quelled when you choose to be compassionate and kind to yourself, forgiving yourself of everything you hold against you. After all, you made the best choices you could make at the time with the information and your state of mind. Things may not pan out, but it doesn't mean you should keep your perceived flaws hanging over your head like a guillotine.

For the Crone: Your shadow self prefers to disconnect from others, isolating herself completely so no one can reach her. You're full of cynicism in this state, never expecting anything good from anyone or any situation. You are too rigid, set in your ways, and unwilling to try something new (even if it could be better than whatever you have going on right now). You have to "find the funny" in life, no matter how dark it may seem. There's always something to laugh at, but you have to be looking for it first. You'll benefit tremendously from accepting that things change and even more so from actively working to create a community of people with a shared vision.

Your cynicism can and should be transmuted into wisdom. A crucial part of wisdom is discernment, which is instrumental in helping you understand who and what to trust. You have this ability within you, and the more you work with it, the more you'll count on yourself. Once you trust yourself, your cynicism will melt because you'll realize that even if others prove to be something other than they seemed initially, you will do the right thing for yourself by walking away and asserting your boundaries. Choose to be flexible. Think about the arbitrary dos and don'ts you've set for yourself and question them. Be willing to learn new ways of being and living. You'll love it.

The World within and the World without

Embodying and expressing your feminine energy highly depends on two environments: the one in your mind and the one around you. You're far more likely to truly express yourself when these two environments are harmonious, allowing you to honor the Divine Feminine. So, here are ways to set up sacred spaces where you can rejuvenate and practice self-reflection:

Creating a space to focus affects your ability to focus.[15]

- **Pick a Spot in Your Home You Can Claim as Your Own:** Choose somewhere everyone knows they must avoid, as it is your private place. This space should have your personal effects and decorations that remind you of your archetype. You may want to decorate it with unique stones, crystals, plants, sculptures, wind chimes, or anything else you feel matches your archetype's vibe. This place must be quiet, or at least it should have an ambient sound that won't distract you from your spiritual and self-reflection practices.

- **Set up an Altar in This Space:** You don't have to if you don't want to, but altars are lovely because they act as an energetic magnet, drawing your focus to your meditation, contemplation, journaling, and rituals while also pulling the Divine Feminine energy so it feels real to you. Your altar could have statues or pictures of the goddesses you are drawn to, precious stones, beautiful flowers, books that hold meaning for you and remind you of who you are, and anything else your heart tells you would fit on it. You could have candles, which should only ever be lit when you can keep an eye on them. Scented candles would be an awesome addition to your altar for a more sensory experience.

- **Prepare Your Mind and Heart:** For your mental and emotional "environment," you should always leave all your troubles behind when it's time to do your work, whether a ritual, shadow work, meditation, or anything else. If you bring said troubles with you, it should be intentional, with the understanding that you will transmute them into better outcomes through your rituals. In other words, you should intend that the Divine Feminine will help you with whatever's bothering you. This intention will help you shift from an energy of fear, anxiety, and worry to peace, gratitude, and trust that the loving Mother Goddess has already sorted it all out.

Before wrapping up this chapter, there's one point to always keep in mind: You will have a more profound connection with the Divine Feminine when you accept that you're worthy. You're worthy of having the gift of life. You're worthy of her love, attention, and other gifts for the simple fact that you exist. You don't need to do, be, or have some extra special, ephemeral quality to experience this energy's reality and love in your life.

Well, there is one thing you must do: Discover your self-worth. By using the practical exercises in this chapter, you'll surely find it. Here's something even cooler: *You'll discover your worth has no end or depth. Your self-worth is infinite.* Begin now by using the advice you've received so far. Begin loving your magnificent self; begin creating as though you could never create badly, and amaze yourself with just how much compassion you can extend to yourself — even when your ego tries to convince you that you're not so hot.

Chapter 4: Sacred Union Within: Balancing Your Energies

Since you now know that the Divine Feminine and the Divine Masculine exist in everyone, and you've begun tapping into the Divine Feminine, it will be easier for you to let the light of the Divine wisdom within you illuminate your path. What happens next? Well, you need to understand the core of each energy, how they play out, and what makes them distinct. Armed with this information, you'll be able to tell when you're out of balance, living a life that skews more toward one energy than the other. Therefore, it will be easier for you to find your center, and as a result, your spiritual growth and general well-being will astound you.

Balance your divine feminine and masculine energies.[16]

The Concept of Duality

Simply observing the world around you should tell you there's something off about the idea that there is only one God that has only masculine attributes. The same oddity should strike you even when you encounter religions or practices claiming this God is truly a goddess and there is none other besides her. Observe life, and you'll find that everything has its polar opposite — although "opposite" is not necessarily the best way to put it.

You see, a thing and its opposite are really one and the same. If you have a dime, just because it has heads and tails doesn't mean you have two dimes. You understand this truth applies to everything in life, even if you have been conscious of it. Seeming opposites are merely the same thing on the extremes of a spectrum.

The same can be said for divinity.

For far too long, many have assumed that God is masculine, but you now understand that God is both masculine and feminine. The creative force responsible for all of life carries the duality mirrored in its creation.

The universe is ruled by cycles and seasons. This progression from cycle to cycle happens even when expressing divinity as masculine or feminine. The Divine Masculine has taken precedence over the Divine Feminine, ruling supreme for at least 25,920 years on Earth. This alternating cycle is real, so much so it has its own name: the Precession of the Equinoxes. Without fail, the Earth journeys through every Zodiac sign, taking at least 2,152 years to move from one sign to the next. By the time this little blue dot completes its journey through every astrological house, at least 25,000 years have passed.

As it turns out, you are fortunate enough to live during a time when the masculine energy is finishing its course and witness humanity's rise to a new level of awareness. In this era, the Age of Aquarius, all souls awaken to a higher and deeper understanding of life they have always carried within but have been unaware of for too long. It is said that this is when the 5th dimension becomes real to everyone. It's when the Divine Feminine and the Divine Masculine express themselves in harmony with one another and every heart and soul. You're already experiencing this transformation, and this book you are reading is evidence.

What Is the Divine Masculine?

The Divine Masculine is a core part of the universe, just as the Divine Feminine is. In the same way that it is impossible to conceive a child without the male and female reproductive cells, it is impossible to conceive a universe without the Divine Masculine and the Divine Feminine working in harmony. You seek to understand what the Divine Masculine is all about. There's no better way to do so than by analyzing its traits.

- **Assertiveness:** The Divine Masculine balances the passivity of the Divine Feminine. Assertion is the quality of doing what needs to be done to get the required results. In the never-ending debate between sexes, assertiveness has often been misconstrued as dominance, but it's not the same thing. Dominance seeks to control through force by any means necessary, with no regard for others, which is toxic masculinity at its finest. It's one way the shadow side of masculine archetypes shows up. It's nothing to do with the Divine Masculine. However, the assertion is about persistence and consistency.

- **Determination:** The Divine Masculine is goal-oriented and relentless in its desire to accomplish set goals. Contrast this with the Divine Feminine, which is laid back, working with emotions and introspection to allow things to come rather than to chase after them. It would be impossible to accomplish your dreams without determination, one of the Divine Masculine's gifts.

- **Action:** The Divine Masculine takes action. It does not remain passive. Passivity is a trait of the Divine Feminine. You can see this mirrored in how men and women relate to one another. In the most traditional sense, the masculine goes after the feminine heart, never stopping until it is secured. Even in nontraditional relationship dynamics, the same holds true. The Divine Masculine energy is about action through movement.

- **Goal-Focused:** The point of the Divine Masculine's action is to accomplish goals. When you are in your masculine energy, you make things happen. You focus on your goals and don't stop until you see them through.

- **Risk-Taking:** Masculine energy is about taking risks, while feminine energy is about remaining safe and pragmatic. There's no way to accomplish your goals if you're not willing to put something on the line, knowing there's a chance this sacrifice may not pay off. Yet, this willingness to take risks is a necessary trait if you are to succeed in life.

- **Protection and Provision:** Where the Divine Feminine nurtures, the Divine Masculine protects. This isn't to imply some foolishness like the term "the weaker sex" holds water. It's the natural role of the Divine Masculine to offer protection. The Divine Masculine naturally sees to it that everyone is provided for through action.

- **Leadership:** The Divine Masculine energy powers leadership. When you have to decide, you're leading, which can only be effectively accomplished when you're in touch with your inner masculine self.

- **Strength and Courage:** Masculinity is about strength in all forms and the willingness to combine that strength with courageous action to accomplish whatever needs to be done despite possible danger or risk.

Signs of Imbalance

When individuals or the human collective lean more toward one divine energy over another, there are unmistakable signs. Look around you. You can clearly see the dark manifestations of the shadow or unhealed aspect of the Divine Masculine. People are stressed, burned out, and unable to find joy in life anymore because they've lost sight of what's important. Perhaps you, too, may have felt this way. How are you in your relationships with others? Do you have trouble setting boundaries, and others walk all over you, or you may disrespect others' boundaries, causing what could otherwise have been a great relationship to become unhealthy and toxic?

People are afraid of being vulnerable these days. They think it's a sign of weakness, so to keep themselves "safe," they repress everything they feel. The result? Everyone walks around in their own little bubbles, isolated from everyone else. The lack of connection is a symptom of a world sorely lacking in empathy, kindness, and compassion. What about the little moments of positivity or the pockets of people who appear to push for a brighter world? Look closer, and you'll find that, in truth, there's nothing "positive" about the positivity brand they push. It's toxic, nothing more than tinsel, a veneer meant to make people shut their pain within even though it eats away at them.

Not having the proper balance between the Divine Masculine and the Divine Feminine energy in your life means you cannot distinguish between your energy and another person's. In other words, you don't have energetic or emotional boundaries, so you take on other people's feelings as if they were yours, which is draining. Even if you are more empathetic than most, you will benefit from learning how to protect your energy and to tell when you're feeling someone else's emotions rather than yours.

The best way to handle this is by deliberately balancing both aspects within yourself. If you don't, you'll find that you abandon yourself emotionally. When you have to express your needs, you don't do so healthily. You want to speak the truth but can't because you're terrified about putting yourself first, even though it's sometimes necessary. Does all this sound familiar?

Another sign is the constant push for productivity, to the detriment of other aspects of your life. Every other influencer or *"furu"* (another way to say "fake guru") yells at you from the YouTube mountains to the TikTok valleys that you must hustle. "You're sleeping too much," is what they say about getting regular hours of sleep. "You're not pushing hard enough," they preach at you, never mind that you've put your blood, sweat, and tears into making these "dreams" you've been sold as the ideal to happen while seeing little to no results - usually due to constantly moving the goalposts. The push for productivity is so bad that people don't take care of themselves anymore. They don't care for their mental or physical health, as they worship at the altar of the almighty dollar in the cathedral of capitalism. Perhaps you, too, are noticing the futility of it all, which is why you've answered the Divine Feminine call.

Things don't look great for the collective either, not when it comes to the imbalance of energies. War is the order of the day. Once upon a time, world leaders would at least put up a facade of caring, as though war were an ugly business they didn't want to be part of but found themselves in the middle of out of necessity. Now? They don't even bother with putting on their makeup and costumes properly. The media's lies are more glaringly obvious than ever, causing an overall feeling of "Us against them."

Even the "us's" have divisions among themselves. This ethos results from having lived far too long, completely ignoring one energy and favoring the other. You may think the solution is a pendulum swing to the other side, to the other extreme where the matriarchy is in charge, and the Divine Feminine is only acknowledged, but that isn't it either. That could easily lead to stagnation, an inability to seek the new and embrace change, and other issues just as bad as being in a world high on spiritual testosterone.

Misconceptions on Balancing the Feminine and Masculine

Here's a quick look at some of the misconceptions people have about what it means to balance the feminine and the masculine:

1. "Balance would lead to everyone being the same, which would make the world a boring place and eventually stagnate progress." This isn't true. There's room for individuality even as people learn to balance both sides. You won't lose yourself, so don't worry.
2. "Once you find balance, you remain in that state for the rest of your life." The truth is you'll always fluctuate in the degree to which you express one energy over another. It's a lifelong practice.
3. "You have to be in a conventional relationship to find this balance." While you can learn a lot about balancing yourself in a relationship, you don't need a partner before you learn to find balance. You're already in a relationship with yourself. Finding a balance between both energies is something you'll do by becoming more self-aware and paying attention to how you relate to yourself.

These are a few misconceptions about balancing the Divine Feminine and Divine Masculine energies. Still, they're some of the more problematic ones that could impede your progress if you believe them. You'll have better physical and mental health by keeping these energies balanced. The power of the divine will become a real, undeniable force in your life you'll learn to rely on for everything you need.

Exercises for Balancing Your Masculine and Feminine Energies

The following techniques and exercises will help you find the balance between your expression of the Divine Feminine and Divine Masculine in your daily life.

Use Breathwork: Breathwork refers to special breathing techniques that alter your state of consciousness and allow you to grasp spiritual ideas better than you would in a regular waking state. It can change your physiology as well as your mind for the better. One useful technique is alternate nostril breathing.

Alternative nostril breathing.[17]

Here's how it works:

1. If you're not already wearing something comfy, do that now.
2. Find a quiet place where you won't be distracted or disturbed. Shut your eyes as you sit in a comfortable position. You'll need about five to 10 minutes of uninterrupted time.
3. Shut your eyes, use your right thumb, and press against your right nostril, shutting off the airflow.
4. With your right nostril shut, take a deep breath through the left one.
5. Release your right nostril so it's open again.

6. Using your ring finger, press down on your left nostril to shut it.
7. Exhale through your right nostril.
8. Repeat this sequence for the next five to 10 minutes.

The beautiful thing about alternate nostril breathing is it helps you balance both hemispheres of your brain, which correlate to the masculine and feminine energies.

Practice Self-Reflective Journaling: This is journaling with a twist. Rather than document what happened each day, write about your feelings concerning the predominant energy you embody. So, even if you write about daily occurrences, do it in the context of how much you express the Divine Feminine and Divine Masculine in balance. As you journal, think about the parts of your life where you sense there might be an imbalance. Pay attention to aspects of your life where you push yourself harder than necessary and find it tough to draw the line with others or express what you need from them. You'll find it helpful to write about your emotions and document how often you were in touch with your intuition and followed it.

Self-reflective journaling should be a daily exercise for effective results.[18]

Get Creative: Creatively expressing yourself is another excellent way to restore the balance between these energies. Consider activities that force you to maintain your focus and discipline your mind or body to channel more of the Divine Masculine. You could learn a new technical skill, play chess, work out, etc. If you sense you could use more of the Divine

Feminine, you should try singing, dancing, writing, painting, sculpting, and other creative endeavors.

Develop Body Awareness: Take up yoga. It is an excellent activity that forces you out of your head and into your body. Certain poses are meant to awaken the Divine Masculine within you, while others will stir the Divine Feminine. An excellent yoga instructor will know how to blend both into a routine.

Reframe Old Wounds: Sometimes, the imbalances of these divine energies are caused by experiences you may have had in the past that traumatized or gave you a mindset that's been a handicap to you. In this instance, it would be most beneficial to dig deep into your past to discover why you've become dependent on one form of energy or the other.

Once you have identified these landmark experiences, you have a new task: You must reframe them to make them positive. You take the negative energy and transmute it using understanding and compassion toward yourself. This doesn't mean you should deny that these things happened or gaslight yourself into thinking that it wasn't that bad. However, you become a researcher keenly on the lookout for the silver linings, the good within the bad. So, how do you find the gold in your pain? By asking yourself what lessons you've learned and how they empower you today.

Let Nature Be Your Ally: The more time you spend in nature, the more balanced you will become because nature does not know how to exist without balance. Whether in your modern spartan apartment several hundreds of floors above the hubbub of humanity and the din of daily life or deep in the heart of the Amazon, you will always be a part of nature. However, deliberately putting yourself in touch with nature accelerates balancing your energies. You can hike, sit on the beach and watch the ocean, walk barefoot on natural ground, lie on your back on the grass, use your imagination, or do whatever else you desire to connect with nature.

Practice Meditation Daily: Meditation may not be easy at first, but it is simple. All you need is five to 10 minutes in a quiet place. Wear comfortable clothing, sit or lie down, and shut your eyes. Keep your attention on your breathing for as long as you can. If you've never done this before, the odds are you will constantly get distracted. This does not mean you're doing anything wrong. It's actually awesome that you are becoming aware of how often your mind jumps from topic to topic. Whenever you notice that you have stopped focusing on your breathing, simply acknowledge whatever thought you have in your mind and gently release it as you return to your breath. You shouldn't be harsh on yourself, even if you get distracted every other second. With consistent practice, you'll become better at maintaining awareness of your thoughts.

Work with Acupuncture and Reiki: Acupuncture can help you get rid of imbalances in the energetic flow in your body's meridians. Reiki is another way to accomplish this by moving stuck energy so there's free flow all through your chakra system and imbalances are sorted out. You'll need to work with a qualified practitioner if you choose to explore these healing modalities to sort out the imbalance between your inner masculine and feminine aspects.

Chapter 5: You're Never Alone — Spirit Guides

Whether or not you've been aware of it, you've never been alone. You've always had divine assistance waiting for you to acknowledge and accept. This help is offered to you by your spirit guides. But who exactly are these beings, and how do they make your life better?

What Are Spirit Guides?

Your spirit guides are precisely what they sound like. They are guides that exist in spirit form, so they are not visible to the naked eye unless you have the gift of an awakened third-eye chakra. In pretty much the same way that air exists but cannot be seen,

You've always had divine assistance waiting for you to acknowledge and accept.[19]

your spirit guides are real, even if you can't see or sense them just yet. As you feel the effect of air, you can pick up on the presence and workings of your guides in your life if you're sensitive to them or become observant. No one knows better than your spirit guides what would serve your highest purpose. No one could possibly offer you better advice than them.

If you are confused because you have multiple options, your spirit guides can give you clarity to help you choose the best path for your intentions. Not only are they excellent advisors, but they also help you to plan, organize, and strategize your life. If you'd like to accomplish something by reaching out to them, they can help you implement your goals. Your spirit guides also play the all-important role of working with the spirit guides of others around you so that the best outcome for everyone is always accomplished — provided you ask for their help. They won't interfere or do anything without your permission because otherwise, their actions would be in violation of your sacred free will.

These amazing beings have been with you ever since you were born, whether or not you were aware of them. Not only do they know your present life like the back of their hands, but they also know your past lives. They understand how all these lives intertwine and affect one another. There's no better source to help you understand the challenges you face and the opportunities you may be missing out on than your spirit guides and their deep well of knowledge. Think of them as energetic encyclopedias on everything concerning your past, present, and future.

Different Kinds of Spirit Guides and Their Roles

Guardian Angels: These guides are known as "life guides" because they accompany you from before birth to after death, from one incarnation to the next. Anytime you feel confused about something, they're there to offer you the best advice. They're the reason you get the sense that you shouldn't be walking down a particular street at a specific time, even if you've always done so with no problems. They give you intuitive nudges to keep you out of trouble and lead you where you want to go.

These beings are like best friends who never judge you and are always there for you. You could argue they're even better than friends because they never take their eyes off you and don't have to sleep or take a day off from work. So, if you're ever in a sticky situation, know that you no longer have to be afraid. You can confirm the reality of these guides by telling them exactly how you want them to help you and watch in amazement as everything you ask for plays out beautifully, thanks to their intervention.

Archangels: The archangels have their work cut out for them across various heavenly realms. They are powerful angels who are not to be trifled with. Why? Because, unlike regular angels and guides, they are tasked with the job of caring for everything affecting every world, known and unknown, seen and unseen. Even in the darkest of times, they ensure humans do not annihilate themselves. They spread their loving kindness and warmth as an energetic shield protecting people from the darkness.

Some people assume because the archangels have a broader scope of affairs to handle, they should never be called on for help. However, this is not the case. You cannot think of these beings as limited in space and time like humans. They can be everywhere, all at once. You are part of the world they care for, so you can call out to them if you're intuitively led to.

Spirit Animals: The interesting thing about spirit animals is that they embody the energy of the animal form they take. Your spirit animal is a source of strength you can draw from whenever you face challenges and tough times. Typically, the spirit animal has a unique quality, resilience, which is necessary for your particular life path. It is not unheard of to have more than one spirit animal or to have your spirit animal change from time to time.

Spirit animals embody energy and strength and guide us.[30]

Of what use are these spirit guides, you wonder? Well, you merely need to think about the attributes of each animal to appreciate what they bring to the table. For instance, the bear has unparalleled strength and the wisdom to hibernate when it's time. The snake is representative of wisdom and regenerative power. The peacock teaches you to show your authentic self fully, with no apologies, and to be proud of who you are. The butterfly is the epitome of the power of transformation. Some people refer to these beings as animal totems. Bringing them to mind or asking for their help will yield good results.

Ancestral Spirits: Your ancestors can also act as spirit guides. They are invested in your affairs because you are their direct descendant. They've had to deal with the same struggles and challenges as you. Since they've already walked your path, they have wisdom and lessons to teach, benefiting you in particular. Your ancestors are an excellent support system. You can draw from their strength and wisdom whenever you need to. Call on them if you feel you could use more courage or bravery. They are fiercely protective of their own. If you choose to interact with your ancestors, it is best to specify that you only want to work with those who have your best interests at heart. Remember, your ancestors were once human, which means, like humans, some may be mischievous at best or downright awful at worst. Why does this matter? Imagine having a serial killer or cult leader as one of your ancestors. Not all ancestors have good intentions. Crossing over to the other side does not necessarily indicate that they have become good people, so you must be specific about who's allowed in your life and who isn't.

Ascended Masters: Once upon a time, ascended masters lived on Earth, just as you do. They've experienced many incarnations and learned so much. They've transcended the need to reincarnate on Earth. Therefore, they serve on a spiritual plane, helping all humanity to navigate life's many challenges. They offer wisdom beyond anything imaginable.

If you connect with ascended masters, they can help you understand your path and how to develop spiritually. These masters have been known to visit people in their dreams, teaching and offering insightful information about specific situations they're experiencing in their waking lives.

Healing Spirits and Messenger Spirits: The spirits' roles are exactly as their names suggest. Healing spirits are there to help you whenever you're mentally, physically, or emotionally down. They revive and rejuvenate your soul, soothing your body, mind, and heart.

As for the messenger spirits, they show up with important pieces of information to help you along your path. Sometimes, they'll use your dreams – and other times, they'll orchestrate engaging experiences that, upon closer inspection, will reveal a deep, meaningful message for you.

Elementals: These are the spirits that are within all of nature. They are in water, fire, air, and Earth. They're in every river, plant, ocean, mountain, etc. They remind you to get in touch with nature, to bring your soul into balance whenever you have lost your way.

Now you know about the many spirit guides available, you should realize that you have access to them all, as they play unique, essential roles in your life.

How Spirit Guides Communicate with You

Spirits always have something for those who have eyes to see and ears to hear. The trouble is that not many people understand when their spirit guides are communicating with them. It's far more common to dismiss their attempts at reaching out as nothing more than mere coincidence. You're not going to make that mistake because you need to hear whatever messages they have for you. Once you become adept at knowing when they're communicating with you and reaching out to them in turn, you can seek their guidance on finding the balance between the Divine Feminine and Divine Masculine in your life. So, here's how to discern that your spirit guides are communicating with you.

You Experience Synchronicity: Synchronicity is the union of a series of unlikely events in time and space in a way that's profoundly meaningful to the person witnessing them. Others may consider these as mere coincidences, but these synchronicities have meaning for you. People in touch with the Divine Spirit understand that there's no such thing as a coincidence. The minute you accept this by default, you'll notice more synchronicity in your life as your guides attempt to reach out to you.

What do these synchronicities look like? You may notice you keep waking up at specific times or looking at the clock just when it has a precise set of numbers, like 11:11 or 4:44. You may see these numbers showing up often on receipts, on license plates, as a perfectly positioned group of football players with their jersey numbers creating that number, etc. You could even hear these numbers in random conversations that have nothing to do with you or turn on the TV just in time to see someone holding up a placard with that number.

Synchronicity could also be a repetition of a certain event in various ways. For instance, Allison reported that she had experienced flooding in her house because of a broken pipe, only for her to get to work the next day and find that the office bathroom had suffered a similar fate. Her guides definitely wanted her to pay attention to something. Curious, she asked for guidance and received her answer in a dream. She was told she would experience a financial emergency but that it was imperative to keep positive through it all because if she did, something wonderful would happen after upgrading her financial status.

The next day, her relative needed to be bailed out, which cost more money than Allison could afford to spare without becoming uncomfortable. Still, she did what she could to help. No less than a week later, this same relative had a windfall after winning the lottery. Feeling gratitude to Allison for bailing her out, she gave her ten times what she'd to bail her out.

Synchronicity also involves receiving answers to questions. You may ask about something bothering you, only to turn on the radio and hear a musician belting out the exact line of the song; that is the perfect, comforting answer. Here's another fun story: Blake feels down about his life and alone. He didn't have anyone he could reach out to due to a terrible falling out he'd had with family and friends resulting from a narcissist's smear campaign. He had a good cry in a café's bathroom and asked for a sign that things would work out fine. When he was done, he splashed water on his face to wash away his tears.

As he opened the door to head back out, another man rushed in, and the two collided, their heads bumping against each other. The man, embarrassed, apologized profusely to Blake, who stood there, staring at the newcomer in awestruck silence. Why? Well, this man wore a T-shirt with these words written in bold lettering: "You'll Never Walk Alone!" To anyone else, that meant nothing. But for Blake, the moment was poignant. As if confirming, a day later, the narcissist who ruined his life was caught in a scandal that unraveled and revealed their many lies, vindicating Blake and restoring his connection with his loved ones.

You Encounter Certain Animals: You usually spot them in the weirdest places, and it feels like they've been waiting there just for you and no one else to find them. They may stare a little longer than an animal ordinarily would at a human.

Encountering animals in weird places can mean that your spirit guides are trying to communicate with you.[21]

You Dream of Your Guides: Guides can show up in your dreams to teach, comfort, warn, clarify, etc. These dreams don't feel ordinary. You wake up with the undeniable knowledge that you met your guide.

They'll Call Your Name or Touch You: Some people have a negative mindset about this, so their belief opens them up to trickster spirits. However, it's not weird to be woken up by your guide softly whispering your name in your ear (or loudly if they have to warn you of something). Sharon's friend Myron had told her that he never needed an alarm clock to wake up since he simply told his guides when he wanted to be up, and he'd be woken at that time or a few minutes before. Sharon thought her friend was nuts, but she was open-minded enough to try. She asked to be woken by 4:30 AM the next day. Sharon was awoken by a warm hand that, in her words, "felt full of love" as it gave her right shoulder a gentle squeeze. She looked at her phone, and sure enough, she watched the digital clock flip from 4:29 to 4:30. Since then, Sharon has actively pursued and developed her connection with her guides.

Your Ears Ring: Contrary to what the skeptics think, this isn't tinnitus. You'll know it because when it happens, there's often something major going on around you, or you may have a thought that was so important your guides had to make you pause to pay attention. Whenever you hear that high-pitched sound, observe what's happening around you and ask yourself what you were thinking of when you heard it. After hearing that sound, follow whatever urge you have because it's your guide leading you away from danger or toward something extraordinary.

How to Develop Your Intuition and Receptivity to Understand Your Guides

You can follow these ten steps to help you tune in to your intuition, which is how your spirit guides reach out to you.

Meditate: Practice meditation every day to train your mind to get to and stay in the state that makes it easy to understand what your guides tell you.

Document Your Dreams: Keep your journal beside your bed. When you wake up, don't move, and don't plan your day in your mind. Instead, think about the last scene or feeling you remember from your dream, then work your way backward. When you can't remember anything more, open your eyes, grab your journal, and write your dreams down. Start with a keyword representing each scene in the dream before filling in the details. This way, you don't forget the rest of your dreams while writing one out. The more you do this, the better your dream recall will be, and the easier it will be for your guides to reach you through your dreams.

Make a List of Things You Want Your Guides to Take Care of: It could have two items or more. When you're done, address them as you would a friend, and ask them to help you handle what you want. Be sincere, respectful, and appreciative of them. The more you do, the stronger the link between you and your guides.

Be Expectant: If you've never done this before, expect that your guides will reach out to you. Don't question it, even if you don't get a response when you think you should. You may not receive an answer or a solution right away, but when you do, you'll find it's right on time and not a moment too soon or too late.

Thank Them Constantly: Think of the things in your life that have improved or are going well. The odds are high that your guides had something to do with it. So, make a point of thanking them each day, not only for what they've done and continue to do, but also for their selfless companionship. Your appreciation is magnetic, drawing your guides closer to you. It fires them up to the point where your conversations and interactions become a moment-to-moment thing.

Before moving on to the next chapter, you should know this: Yes, many naysayers say spirit guides are nothing more than a figment of imagination that desperately needs to be checked. However, there's only one way to refute these skeptical attacks. By putting everything you've learned here to work. Be prepared to be wowed by the reality of your guides. Think about what you hope to gain from this wonderful partnership you're about to become a conscious part of, and you're bound to succeed. Prioritize asking for their help balancing the Divine Feminine and Divine Masculine in your life. You won't be disappointed.

Chapter 6: Connecting with Your Allies

You now have the most relevant information about your spirit guides. So, it's time to get your hands in the clay and discover how you can establish a connection with these wonderful beings. In this chapter, you'll learn to sustain that connection even when life's vicissitudes attempt to pull you away from your spiritual relationships with these guides.

Connect with your spirit guides.[22]

Preparing Your Mind and Spirit

If you've spent most of your life blissfully unaware of spiritual reality, you need to work on getting into the correct state of mind and spirit before connecting with your guides. Why does this matter? Skipping this important process would be like trying to see through glasses with lenses smeared with oil and dirt or eavesdrop on a conversation three rooms away while loud heavy metal music is blasted from massive speakers.

The oil, dirt, and metal music refer to the many beliefs and biases society has installed in your mind about the nature of reality, the existence of worlds beyond the physically observable one, and the feasibility of establishing contact with beings that, according to science, logic, and reason, don't exist.

One of the biggest mistakes you could make in grasping a spiritual concept like the Divine Feminine is to curve-fit spirit to matter. In other words, you cannot use physical rules and expectations as a basis to determine that spirituality is nonexistent hogwash. Many realize there's something off about the stories they've been fed since birth. Perhaps you were one of these people. Perhaps in the past, you noticed every time you had a question that would shatter your illusions about how reality works, you would get a spiritual or mental pop-up blocker, for lack of a better way to describe it.

This pop-up blocker is a carefully crafted line of logic or reason that immediately causes you to shut down your spiritual exploration. One of the most effective blockers is the "fact" that if it cannot be observed by the five senses or picked up by a scientific instrument, it must not exist. This is an arrogant approach to understanding things beyond the physical. It would be like using a thermometer to check the volume of sound or a noise meter to detect the temperature of water. In other words, how can you use physical instruments to measure or determine the existence of spiritual realities? Some things lie beyond the rigid straight lines of reason and logic —necessary for operating in this physical world but not in realms beyond. Until you are willing to accept this, you will not make much progress.

Two of the quickest ways to break through the persistent illusion of lies you've been sold is to practice meditation, which will increase your self-awareness, and to question everything, including your own thoughts — especially those you are 100% certain are true. Do not listen to derogatory, dismissive statements like "It's all in your head." The truth is, it really all is in your head, including your experience of the physical world. There is no way to perceive reality, physical or spiritual, other than through your awareness or consciousness. Quantum physicists are closer to this truth than other scientists. But that's not a matter to be concerned about; they will catch up eventually.

Now that you have the premise needed to experience your spirit guide's reality, you have to put in the work. The first step is to assume that what you have learned here is true and that you can experience it. You do not need to use logic or reason to justify this assumption because the odds are with your programming (especially if you grew up in the Western world rather than Africa or the East, where spirituality isn't scoffed at and is consciously experienced every day), you may be too doubtful to initiate the first contact with your guides.

So, pause for a moment and assume that the version of you who questioned spiritual affairs never existed, assuming that you've always understood the reality of things beyond what is observable with the physical senses. Done? Good. Here are other things to prepare your mind and spirit to commune with your guides.

Keep Your Mind Focused on Your Goal: More than anything else, you should hunger for a connection with the Divine. To sustain that hunger and passion for connecting with what is beyond you, you should do everything within your power to remind yourself of how important this goal is to you. If it means setting alarms throughout the day to remind you to check in with yourself, meditating, contemplating the existence of spiritual guides, or checking in with them, do it. An excellent way to ensure you remain focused is to set things up so that connecting with your spirit guides is the first thing on your mind in the morning and the last thing when you go to bed at night.

Set Your Intentions and Make Them as Clear as You Can: Some people ask for signs that their spirit guides exist, and that's all they ever get - signs and nothing more. However, if you want constant, ongoing dialogue between yourself and your spirit guides, you should be clear about that. The clearer you are about your intentions for establishing contact with your guides, the better your results will be.

You cannot ask for signs and then be upset when all you ever get is a barrage of 444s and 1111s. You must be clear about what you want. If you haven't figured it out yet, there's no rush. Take your time to create your intention to the letter, and then you may begin the process knowing that you'll achieve your spiritual goal in a matter of time.

Stay Open and Receptive: With your focus on your goal and your intentions crystal clear, you'll notice moments when you have an extra sense of presence and awareness. Some people have mistaken this for depersonalization or derealization, but that's not what it is. It's your spirit guides bringing the fullness of your awareness to the here and now. You cannot connect with them in your past or your future. You can only establish that connection in the now.

When you become more aware and present, you'll find it easier to let them help you. You'll hear them, and that's good because they're always ready to speak with you. However, if you shake off the feeling of "extra presence," you close yourself off from your guides. So, rather find a quiet place every time you feel this way and sit in silent meditation and expectation for at least fifteen minutes. Don't sit aimlessly. Instead, set an intention to receive and understand your guide's message clearly.

Guided Visualization to Initiate Contact with Your Guides

One of the best things to connect with your spiritual guides is to meditate daily. You can use the alternate breathing technique regularly to help you. Whatever you choose, always set your intention for the technique before you begin. Now, on to another powerful, potent tool to help you make your spirit guides as real as the words on this page.

Guided visualization is like meditation but with instructions. You can write and record your guided visualizations, but if you prefer, you could use one available for free online. The idea is that you will not merely be meditating but focusing on the instructions about what to do with your body and what to imagine as you meditate. Here is a simple one you can use right now. Since you cannot meditate while reading, record this first. Don't rush your recording so you have time to follow each instruction. When you're ready to use the guided visualization, ensure you're dressed comfortably and in a quiet space where you won't be disturbed. Switch off all devices. If you don't live alone, ask your people not to bother you until you let them know you're ready.

Instructions:
1. Sit on a chair or the mat.
2. Feel your body. Make adjustments until you feel comfortable, then close your eyes.
3. Now you're settled, part your lips slightly. You're going to breathe deeply in through your nose and out through your mouth. Your

exhales may be longer than your inhales, and that's okay. For now, just enjoy breathing, allowing your body to flood with love and light as you inhale and allow it to relax as you exhale.

4. Notice how, with each breath, you sink deeper and deeper into your body, feeling relaxed and at ease, very present in the moment.
5. Now that your body is settled and your mind is quiet, imagine a beautiful place. It has to be somewhere that calls to you. It could be a mountain top, a beach, a garden, or a forest. It could be your childhood home or a particular time and place when you felt safest.
6. Imagine yourself walking down the path that leads to this peaceful place. Pay attention to the crunch beneath your feet as each hits the floor.
7. As you walk, you notice up ahead of you there's a figure. Something about them draws you. With each step, you feel the love coming from them toward you. This being is your spirit guide. There's no specific form your guide needs to take on. They'll choose something familiar and comfortable, so you needn't fear or worry.
8. As you draw closer, notice what they're wearing and how they look. Are they smiling? How do their eyes make you feel as they look upon you?
9. Now, you're slow to a stop as you stand before your guide. Their arms are spread out, beckoning you to hug them. You accept their invitation and embrace them, feeling the warmth, love, and light flowing from them into your body, mind, and spirit.
10. Now, you pull back and thank them for their presence. If you have any questions, you ask them and wait with them as they speak to you. They may simply project thoughts into your mind if they don't use words. If what you receive in response feels more like energy or an emotion, you can trust that the matter you've brought forward is already resolved. You'll see or receive a clear answer in the days to come.
11. Offer your guide sincere thanks for their presence, support, and comfort. Embrace them once more. When you're ready, return your awareness to your body and how it feels. Notice your breath once more.
12. In five seconds, you will open your eyes feeling refreshed and rejuvenated, with your heart and mind at peace.

13. You're becoming more and more aware of your breath.
14. Your awareness of your body is increasing.
15. Now you're noticing the space you're in, becoming aware of sounds and sensations.
16. You're stirring, waking up.
17. You're fully present, joyful, and energized. Gently open your eyes.

What If You Can't Imagine? Some people don't have the ability to see things in their mind's eye. If this is you, no worries. You can still use guided visualization, but instead of trying to imagine a physical place, transport yourself mentally to a time in the past when you felt safe and hold on to the feeling. In other words, forget about visuals and focus on sensations, emotions, and sound.

Signs and Confirmations

As mentioned, your spirit guides are always ready to speak to you. Trust is essential if you intend to fully comprehend whatever they're sharing with you. You have to trust that your guides exist. Trust in the process of initiating contact, whether through meditation, guided visualization, or breathwork. Finally, trust they will make themselves known to you, should you intend it. Here are the signs you're developing a strong connection with your guides:

Repeated number sequences are one form of synchronicity you may see.[28]

1. You see more synchronicities in your life, especially with the repeated number sequences.
2. Sometimes, you're awoken in the middle of the night, and a clear voice is speaking within you that isn't your usual mental voice.

3. You have an inner knowing that your guide is present.
4. You experience interesting phenomena like books falling off shelves for no reason.
5. You come across the same message multiple times from various unconnected sources.
6. The area between your eyebrows tingles and pulses. This is your third eye or ajna chakra.
7. You're receiving more and more unique ideas.
8. Your dreams become more vivid, last longer, and appear to have a real-time feeling rather than the illogical shift from one scene to the next typical of dreams.
9. You get the sense that you're not alone — not figuratively, but literally.
10. You feel physical sensations like touch, inexplicable and illogical shifts in temperature, etc.
11. You get a tingling sensation at the back of your neck, toward the base.

If you'd like to be confident that you genuinely are establishing contact with your guides, you'll find it beneficial to journal every extraordinary experience. You should ensure you're being truly guided and not merely assuming your interpretation of a situation is from your spirit guides. The best way to be certain is through constant observation. Become a scientist, noting everything you receive and comparing and contrasting events.

Do not share what you're up to with people who will likely look at you as if you're doing "woo-woo stuff" because they'll probably think you're crazy. You may presume they're right when they aren't. You can let others know later (only if you're inspired to) when you've developed trust and have connected with your guides often enough to be convinced they're real. You can't be shaken at that point because you have proof of your experiences to back up your claim. You now trust your intuition.

Skeptics will belittle your conviction by referring to your lived experiences as "anecdotal evidence only," but don't let that bother you. Think of it like trying to explain to someone from the Stone Age that a small little device held in the palm of your hand can help you pinpoint exactly where you are on Earth or watch silly cat videos. They'd find it hard to believe if they didn't see it themselves!

In the meantime, journaling will help you track the patterns and understand when your guides are present. Also, it is an excellent tool for keeping your mind focused on establishing contact. Another thing you should do is check in with those who understand the reality of spirit guides so they can offer helpful pointers.

Chapter 7: Cultivating Deeper Bonds

Some people are satisfied with surface-level manifestations of spiritual matters. They are content with seeing license plate numbers and digital displays with synchronistic or "angel" numbers, but they aren't too keen on seeing how deep the rabbit hole goes. The fact that you're reading this book implies you want more for yourself than that. This is commendable because many benefits are had from developing a deeper connection with your spirit guides. By strengthening and deepening your bond with these beings, you will experience transformation for the better across every aspect of your life.

Deepen your bond with your spirit guides.[34]

The Core Essence of Developing a Deeper Connection

What's the whole point of wanting to deepen your connection with your spirit guides? Well, the business of life is not easy to navigate, so it certainly helps to have access to your inner wisdom on command. The deeper your connection with your spiritual side, the easier it is to connect with your guides, who will offer profound information that could only be classified as wisdom. They'll communicate using dreams, synchronicity, intuition, and other means necessary. Many people wake up each day feeling lost and confused. They live their lives in a haze. They have no idea what they want to do. However, as a person with a deep bond with your spirit guides, you will never have to deal with the torture of confusion. You will be aware of your true purpose in life because you have access to unparalleled guidance.

The ultimate goal of developing a powerful tie with your spirit guides is to help you embrace the Divine Feminine energy. They'll offer guidance to help you break the shackles of limiting beliefs and perspectives that have made it impossible to allow the Divine Mother's love and light to flow through your life. Your spirit guides can help you develop a broader perspective, showing you how many more choices you have than you previously assumed. For instance, if you're struggling in your relationships, they'll show you how to love yourself. Once you do, you'll realize you never had to struggle or beg to be loved, and the right love will come your way through more paths than one. Or have you always assumed there's only one way to earn a living? Your guides can open your eyes to show you unlimited potential, revealing opportunities for abundance you may have overlooked all this time. They will show you how to access the Divine Mother's benevolence.

Saved By Her Guide

Kachi had been planning a trip to Spain for a long time. She dreamed of visiting the country for her whole life and fantasized about walking down the beautiful Paleo de la Castellana and the Calle de Preciados. When she'd finally saved enough money and could take her vacation, she was beyond ecstatic. So, imagine what she must have felt like when she had the dream the night before. Her guide, who she was used to meeting in dreams, had shown up.

Wordlessly, he took her hand, and the scene became the airport. They were standing on the asphalt, watching a plane take flight. The scene shifted again. This time, Kachi and her guide were in the clouds above the plane. They watched as it crashed.

Then, Kachi was awake, but her eyes were still shut. On her bed, she felt her hand being urgently squeezed. It was the same hand the guide held in her dreams. She got the message, "Don't go." Kachi was miffed, but she wasn't about to disobey her guide. She tried to call the airline to warn them about the imminent crash, but no one took her seriously. After all, people played pranks like this all the time, and if the airline kept grounding planes, they'd soon be out of business. There was nothing further she could do. That night, she watched the news coverage of the plane crash her guide saved her from. This is just one of many ways your guide can help you.

A Financial Turnaround

Jeremy was a simple person who never believed in spiritual concepts. As a man who had to work multiple jobs to survive, he did the best he could, but he felt that his life lacked meaning. A series of events would eventually lead him to discover that spirit guides are real. So, he took a leap of faith to contact his spirit guide.

From that point forward, Jeremy began to find reasons to get out of bed in the morning other than to survive. He was more than happy to explore the teachings his guides offered him, and he could see how his emotional well-being improved. However, he wanted his financial life to improve, and so he brought the matter forward in meditation.

Jeremy knew next to nothing about finances or how to manage money, so rather than be specific about how he wanted help, he simply told his guides to help him in whatever ways they felt best. His social media was constantly flooded with messages about how to be your own boss, but he never believed he was cut out for that.

Three days after Jeremy set his intention for financial success, he was fired from two of his jobs. The week after, the remaining business he worked for shut down because the owners declared bankruptcy. Jeremy was confused. After all, he had asked his guides for assistance with his finances. Instead, he had lost all earning power. Downcast, he revisited the matter with his guides in a meditation session. He received one word in response to his query, "Trust."

Moments later, his friend Michaela knocked on his door. As they spoke, Michaela mentioned she was taking a class on trading cryptocurrency. Having watched too many YouTube videos on cryptocurrency scams, trading them was the last thing Jeremy thought to give his attention. Yet there was a palpable electricity in the air as soon as the words left Michaela's mouth. For Jeremy, time stood still. Once more, he got the message internally, "Trust."

Fast forward a few months later, and Jeremy is doing phenomenally well as a cryptocurrency trader, making his monthly salary in a matter of weeks and compounding his profits. If his guides hadn't gotten him out of his job, he wouldn't have had the time or focus to learn this new skill that did more than pay the bills and let him survive.

Setting Time Aside for Spirit

If you want to get better at something, you need to practice consistently. Set aside time each day to engage in your spiritual practices to help you get a stronger connection with your guides. How can you pull this off?

1. Before arbitrarily picking a time, try different times of the day. Some people feel much better when they practice first thing in the morning, others last thing at night, and others may prefer the middle of their day. It all comes down to your schedule and where you can find room for your guides. If you have the time, you could carve out at least 10 minutes thrice a day for your practice, but if you don't, 10 to 15 minutes once a day at the same time is optimum.

2. If you're unaccustomed to meditating or focusing on something for a while, you should start with shorter durations. Once more, 10 to 15 minutes is a good starting point. As you progress, you may naturally notice you're giving more and more time than usual to your practice. If you have a hard time lasting longer, work your way up from 15 minutes to 20 minutes gradually. When you become comfortable focusing for 20 minutes on your spiritual practice, you can ramp it up to 25 minutes. Keep adding five minutes each time you notice you can sit still without being as distracted as you used to be.

3. Think of your spiritual practices, like brushing your teeth. They're not optional or negotiable. Your decision has nothing to do with your feelings. You will still clean your teeth whether or not you see

gunk on them or if you're happy or sad. Use the same approach in your spiritual life. With this mindset, you will never be tempted to skip a day. You'll do what you should, regardless of whether you feel in the mood or not.

4. Working with more than one tool to connect with your guides? Get organized by assigning a set time to each practice. Note that there may be certain times when your guides have so much to do with you. At times like these, you should allow flexibility so that you do not interrupt the process. When that's not the case, work with your set schedule.

Personalizing Your Rituals

You could look up already-established rituals people use to connect with your spirit guides. However, it would be of greater benefit to create your own. Crafting your own ritual means working with your intuition, which is one way your guides communicate with you. Since they know you better than anyone else, they will know what elements to include and what actions you need to perform to establish a greater connection between you than if you went with someone else's methods. The process will give you a sense of empowerment because it will convince you that you can communicate with your spirit directly without an intermediary's help. So, now you understand the necessity for personalizing your rituals. Here are five ideas to help you with the process:

1. Consider making offerings to your guides at the start of your rituals to demonstrate your gratitude.
2. Add nature to your practices when and where possible. You could work with specific plants and stones, representations of animals, and elements like sunlight, moonlight, rainwater, etc.
3. You can work your rituals into your breakfast, lunch, or dinner. Think of it like having a meal with your guides.
4. If you're a music lover, incorporating music into your rituals is an excellent way to deepen your experience. You could chant, hum, or play ambient music that puts you in the mood.
5. Incense is another excellent addition to help you banish unwanted or stale energy in your spiritual space and amplify your guide's energy.
6. Make the lighting in your ritual space softer, and you'll connect with your guides more easily.

Alternative Modalities for Connecting with Your Guides

Oracle Cards: These cards have lovely pictures and words printed on them. You can work with them to get more clarity on what your guides are communicating to you. When you have your decks ready, begin by thanking your guides and letting them know what you'd like guidance on and that you want clear messages that are impossible to misunderstand. Then, shuffle the cards while you ask the question.

Oracle cards can help you get more clarity on what your guides are communicating to you.[25]

When your intuition leads you to stop shuffling, pull out a card. These cards often come with interpretations so you can get a general idea of the answer you're receiving. Then, sit in silence to see what else your guides will share to offer further clarity.

If you don't get anything extra but still need reassurance, state the intention while shuffling the cards once more, stop shuffling when you're led to, and pull out another card. This card will clarify your answer. When you're done, you can write the insights you received in your journal to review later.

Dreamwork: This modality is excellent for getting clarity, confirmation, healing, miracles, and more from your guides. How does it work? Firstly, before you go to bed, you have to set your intention that you would like to connect with your guide in your dream. You can state this intention aloud or say it in your mind. A simple sentence will suffice.

You need a journal dedicated to recording your dreams and their interpretations. If you're accustomed to waking up during the night, you should always bring your intention to mind rather than hurry to open your eyes or roll out of bed. Dreamwork is impossible without good dream recall. How can you get better at remembering your dreams?

1. When you wake up from a dream, whatever you do, don't open your eyes and don't move your body. If you do, the odds are high that you will forget your dreams.
2. When you go to bed, practice recalling everything you did that day by starting with the last thing you did before getting into bed. In the beginning, this won't be easy to accomplish, but with time and practice, you'll get better.
3. When you have dreams, you use the same method of recalling the last thing you saw or felt when you were in the dream, then moving backward from there. You may lose all recollection if you attempt to remember the first thing you dreamt.
4. Take reality checks throughout your day. For instance, you could look at a clock, look away, and then look at it again. If you notice the time is still the same, you're definitely not dreaming. In dreams, the time tends to waver. The same can be said for all written text. Another excellent check is to bounce your feet against the floor and see if you hover or fly. Also, ask yourself what you were doing before, whatever you're doing now, and keep working your way backward. This works because if you do it in a dream, you'll catch on that there's something odd about going from your living room to the Eiffel Tower when you actually live in New Jersey. The more you perform these reality checks, the more likely those habits will spill over into your dreams. When you do the checks and realize you're dreaming, you can become lucid and ask your guide to come to you.

Automatic Writing: When you practice automatic writing, you're not thinking about the words coming through. You simply allow them to flow from the pen onto the paper, trusting that the messages come directly from your spirit guides. You first need to set an intention about what you want guidance on. Next, get into a meditative state. When you arrive at the point where your mind and body are still and in the moment, you may write. Don't overthink what comes out of you. Don't try to edit it. If it is gibberish, allow it. As you continue, your words will eventually take on meaning and offer you a profound perspective on whatever you want to know. When you're done, thank your guides for coming through and reviewing what you've received so you can internalize it.

Chapter 8: Meditative Pathways: Accessing Higher Consciousness

There is no better way to attain higher consciousness than through meditation. Far too many people are stuck worrying about the future or regretting their past to focus on the present. Remaining in the here and now is a prerequisite for attaining higher consciousness. In this chapter, you'll learn everything about the different forms of meditation and how to use them to access this higher consciousness, which will positively affect your life.

Mediation leads to a higher state of consciousness.[26]

What Is Higher Consciousness?

Higher consciousness is a concept covering multiple principles. The first thing you need to understand about the state of consciousness is that it sets you free from the idea of limitation and lack. As Bashar (channeled by Darryl Anka) once said, there is no such thing as lack — only an abundance of lack because abundance is all there is. This may sound like gibberish and "copium" to those who haven't woken up yet. However, there is truth to that statement. By developing your connection to higher consciousness and keeping it open, you will experience this truth in real-time. Nothing gives you peace of mind quite like the understanding that higher consciousness offers you.

Higher consciousness is about an expanded state of awareness. It is about perceiving things outside the purview of the physical world or anything your five senses can distinguish. When you operate from a state of higher consciousness, you realize that attempting to fix your life through action alone is like looking at your reflection in a mirror and manipulating its lips with your fingers, hoping it'll smile. Higher consciousness is understanding that all things come from awareness of being first. In other words, if you want that reflection to smile, you're going to have to smile, and only then will you see what you want to see. Higher consciousness is about being, not doing. Whatever you want to accomplish or become, you must first be it. How do you pull this off?

First, you must accept that the version of you who has accomplished what you want already exists as you. Then, assume you are that person and operate from that perspective. As someone who's in touch with a higher consciousness, you are a self-aware person who understands how you feel, why you feel the way you do, how those feelings affect your thoughts, and how they come together to motivate you to take action. You understand the interrelationship between thoughts, emotions, and actions.

It is impossible to be in this heightened sense of awareness without having a sense of empathy and acting on it compassionately. You do not see any distinction between yourself and the next person from this state. Jesus was explaining this to his disciples by saying that as they helped others around them, they were really helping him. Higher consciousness is knowing that you and the others are the same. This knowledge does wonders for your creativity and intuition because you'll find it easy to tap into the "spiritual internet" and draw from the collective conscious or unconscious whatever new ideas you seek to create, understand, heal, grow, or make other intentions real.

Benefits of Accessing Higher Consciousness

Peace of Mind: One of the greatest gifts of higher consciousness is that it keeps you in the present moment. In other words, if you are a very anxious person, constantly worried and depressed, embodying the higher consciousness ideal of being here and now will sort out your issues, giving you what is described as "the peace that passes all understanding."

A Broader Range of Perception: Your connection with higher consciousness means you can pick up on information inaccessible to most because they do not operate through any other modality than the physical. They rely too heavily on what their five senses tell them. Did you know that sunlight gets to you 500 seconds late? Did you also know that what is observed depends on the observer's state of mind? This begs the question, what is the ultimate reality?

The answer is there is an infinite number of possibilities. It's a matter of choosing which of these possibilities you prefer. For instance, if you'd like to become financially successful, it doesn't matter that you've never experienced this as an objective physical reality. It also doesn't matter that your current reality does not match what you'd prefer. By remaining in the state of higher consciousness, you manifest your desired ideal by assuming you are already a financially successful person. Then, the physical world — a delayed mirror of your assumptions about who you are until the point of changing them — will have to show you evidence of your new state of consciousness or being in due time.

Stronger Intuition: Some people only ever receive intuitive messages when in extreme need or danger. What if you could remain in constant contact with your intuition at every point in time? This is an essential benefit that accessing higher consciousness offers you. Think of it like having an eye in the sky, helping you bypass obstacles and threats, and leading you through the shortest and best paths to wherever you want.

In truth, the benefits of accessing higher consciousness are endless. Your life will once more be flooded with meaning and purpose so that you look forward to each new day. You'll develop a stronger backbone, able to handle whatever life throws at you because you understand that all roads lead to your greatest good. You'll have better problem-solving skills on account of how much more creative you are thanks to this infinite well of creativity that is higher consciousness.

What's more, the relationship between you and yourself will take a turn for the better, helping you realize your power, value, and worth. Your relationships with others will also become richer, with every moment offering up a new, more amazing gift than the last as you commune with the people in your life.

Meditation

Meditation is about so much more than trying to relax or destress. These days, clear capitalism has sunk its talons once more into something originally meant to help humanity. Look it up, and you'll find someone's trying to sell you an app, scented candles, a subscription course, or something else often packaged in a way that strips the essence from the concept to make it easier to sell. After all, it's easier to market speed and ease, a silver bullet, a quick fix.

Meditation is a practice requiring commitment and the willingness to maintain focused awareness. You do it on your own while sitting or reclining in a semi-upright position. Group meditations are also possible, but in connecting with your Divine Feminine, you should meditate on your own to learn to focus on a single thing without getting distracted.

Meditation isn't just something you do when you feel you need to unwind. Sure, it works for that purpose. But if you want to go beyond focused attention and deep relaxation to an altered state of consciousness where you perceive the reality that it powers, you can do so with meditation. It's a tool that leads to greater mindfulness. You can use it as a gateway to the many worlds within you and to connect directly to higher consciousness.

Even science has caught on that there's much more to meditation than sitting in silence and accomplishing nothing. A study by the University of the Sunshine Coast revealed that you develop better attention with mindfulness. The researchers worked with 81 participants at least 60 years old, getting them involved in mindfulness, and they were examined six months later. The meditators had improved immensely at keeping their attention on one thing from the changes in their brain structure resulting from their eight-week practice. They also found that people who meditate or use other mindfulness practices get better at processing information through their five senses as their perception becomes sharper. Some findings clearly demonstrate that mindfulness makes the brain more malleable and open to changing and developing for the better, as meditation causes neuroplasticity.

Types of Meditation

You can choose from a plethora of meditation techniques, depending on your goals. Some are dynamic, meaning you have to walk or move to do them. There's no such thing as one form of meditation being superior to others. It's best to try them and keep doing what resonates with you the best. Some meditations require keeping your attention on a specific thing throughout, like a candle's flame, a spot on the wall, the sound of dripping water, a smell, your breath, a mantra, etc. With time, you'll sustain your attention without getting distracted, and when you lose track, you're quick to return your attention to the object you're focusing on.

There's open monitoring meditation, where you allow your attention to wander while remaining detached from what you perceive on the inside or the outside. You don't judge anything but perceive all things as they are. You remain non-reactive. Then there's effortless presence, where your attention isn't on any specific thing. Your only focus is on being here now. Arguably, you could think of this meditation as the ultimate meditation, getting to the point of silence and formlessness where you're everything and nothing. That sentence will make more sense as you practice. With these general groupings in mind, here are specific techniques you could try:

Zen Meditation: Sit on the floor using a cushion or a mat with your legs crossed in lotus or half lotus. You can sit on a chair. Just ensure your spine is straight. You remain focused on your breath as it goes in and out through your nostrils, counting your breath and starting the count over when you're distracted. Alternatively, you can simply sit, be here now, and observe what's popping up in your mind and what's happening in your environment without overthinking anything.

Vipassana: First, you have to learn to concentrate, which comes from basic meditation, where you notice your breath, whether it's the feeling of air flowing through your nostrils or the rise and fall of your stomach. This is your primary focus. Stick with it, and other things will arise for you to notice, whether in your body or via thought. When you feel this new element has taken your attention away from your primary focus, give it a moment more, and label it in your mind with a suitable word that describes it, like "smelling," "desiring," "thinking," "remembering," etc. It should be a general word. There's no need for detailed labeling. Rather than label a sound "airplane," "TV," or "laughter," choose "hearing." Rather than "headache," "cramps," or "pins and needs," use "sensation." In place of anger, joy, confusion, etc., "feeling" will do. When you label the thing, turn your attention back to the primary focus.

Mantra Meditation: A mantra is a sound that may or may not have meaning. It could be a word or a series of words. To perform the mantra meditation, sit in silence and begin chanting it by repeating it aloud or in your mind. If you do it aloud, you'll notice subtle vibrations moving through you. There may be times when you don't want to chant aloud, then do so in your mind. Here are some of the most common mantras:

- Om
- Yam
- Ham
- So, ham
- Rama
- Om namah Shivaya
- Om Shanti
- Om mani padme hum
- Hu
- Brzee

You can repeat your chosen mantra 108 times or 1008 - or set a timer and keep chanting until it goes off!

Practical Tips for Effective, Regular Meditation

1. Always set an intention for your meditation before you begin. If you want to relax, set that intention. If you want to go further, lock that in your mind first.
2. You should always meditate somewhere free from distractions, especially when you're just starting. After a while, you'll find you can meditate even in the middle of a busy, noisy street or on the dancefloor in a nightclub — if there's ever a reason you have to meditate in those places.

3. Select a meditation method you resonate with. If something doesn't work for you, move on to something else.
4. Your meditation experience will be deeper if you take the time to set up the ambiance and make your space sacred. Soft lighting, candlelight, incense, and natural elements are excellent ways to make your space more sacred.

The Challenges and Rewards of Living with Higher Consciousness

It would be remiss of this book not to enlighten you of the challenges you will face when you choose to live a life full of higher consciousness. You'll become more aware of sensations, receiving extra information from sources other than your five physical ones. This may be overwhelming for the beginner who is only becoming deliberate about pursuing their spiritual growth. If you ever feel this way, you'll find it helpful to ground yourself in reality. Take a walk in nature, or spend time in it. If you can walk barefoot on natural ground, do that. You could practice scanning your body, working from your feet up to your head, and being aware of how the muscles feel in each part. Also, be firm with your boundaries because your practice may draw individuals who want to take advantage of your fresh energy.

Additionally, sometimes it will feel like you're taking a step forward only to take several backward because you're coming up against the roots of the patterns you've unconsciously executed without thought. You'll come face to face with your ego, which doesn't want you to continue on this path because it fears you'll see it for what it is: an illusion, and it will die. The fix here is to be compassionate toward yourself as you deal with the internal push and pull. Accept that this feeling is part of the dance of spiritual evolution.

Spiritual evolution can be a lonely journey, as not many people are prepared to deprogram themselves as you're doing. You may lose old friends and experience distance between you and your family. Seek out people working consciously on their spiritual growth, just like you, so you don't feel alone and will be encouraged to continue being your authentic self.

The rewards of living a life of higher consciousness far outweigh whatever downsides you may imagine. Nothing in the world could offer you the amount of inner peace that this modality of life can. The sands of time and space may shift under your feet, but you're not shaken because higher consciousness is the ultimate foundation of all life, so you know you won't fall. You can trust in its stability. You become part of those souls who are getting in touch with their compassionate, empathetic sides and sharing that warmth and love with a world in sore need of healing and peace. You become more intuitive and creative, living a life where every breath you take is pregnant with purpose and passion, a life where you realize the only things that matter are here, now, and how you occupy this space and time.

Chapter 9: Prayer as a Sacred Ritual

What Is Prayer?

Prayer is universal. It is communicating with the Divine, with that which is beyond comprehension, regardless of what you call it or how you interact with the force. It's invoking the power of the source of all life, channeling it toward achieving a goal. It's showing appreciation and, when needed, seeking intervention to change something in your life or another's for the better. Typically, people pray to their ancestors, deities, or whatever versions of God they believe in. Prayer isn't only about asking for things but also being thankful and offering praise in words and with rituals and offerings. Prayer isn't like regular communication because you're connecting with a power that is anything but physical.

Prayer is communication with the Divine.[27]

People have always prayed, whether or not they fully understand what or who they're praying to. You can pray on your own or as part of a group. For some, prayer is the performance of rituals, and for others, prayer involves singing hymns, chanting incantations, and stating personal credos. Every religion in the world practices prayer in some form. With certain ideologies, prayer is something strict, with a set of rules that must be followed to the letter. For others, there's more room for creative flow, allowing you to go with your intuition. Generally, prayer has a dual nature. How? You speak to the Divine, but also, you listen. You ask in prayer, and you receive.

Science has looked into prayer and its power, specifically to see how it can lead to healing, but as usual, its results are contradictory. On the one hand, some scientists approach their research with a bias against all things spiritual, which inevitably affects their interpretation and experience of prayer. On the other hand, charlatans like cult leaders and faux prosperity preachers have weaponized their charisma to control people unwilling to think for themselves and are susceptible to being brainwashed. These people fake miracles and more, and inevitably, once scientists set their sights on them to investigate, they walk away from their studies, even more convinced that prayer is a pointless hoax.

Prayer through the Lens of Traditions and Religions

Look into the Abrahamic religions, and you'll find that prayer has always played a significant role. God's faithful followers would communicate with him through prayer, usually spontaneously, and often on their own, in the Hebraic Bible — until things changed at the start of the book of Deuteronomy, where rules and structure for prayer were laid. In the pages of the New Testament, you'll find that the prayers were more about commanding good things to happen, like healing, deliverance from demons, resurrection, etc. The Christians of those times learned to make prayer a regular thing and to do it privately. The Lord's Prayer was an excellent example that Jesus offered the people to use.

Prayer plays a significant role in the Abrahamic religions.[28]

What about Judaism? Thrice a day, you must observe your prayers — the Shacharit, Mincha, and Ma'ariv. Certain religious ceremonies have much longer prayers. Generally, the Jewish prayers have two parts: the intention (or *kavanah*) and the organized aspects (the *keva*). One of the Jews' most common prayers is the *Amidah*, "The Standing Prayer." Then there are the Kabbalists, who pray with kavanot - which are *intentions tied to their prayers,* meant to ensure a swift and effective answer in response.

The Muslims call prayer *salah*, an Arabic word referring to the prayers that must be made five times daily at set times. Every Muslim knows to pray to face the direction of Mecca's Kaaba once they hear the adhan, the "call for prayer." They often begin their prayers with praise for God and his greatness. They will read portions of the Quran during their sessions, honor God by lowering themselves to the ground in prostration or sujud, and offer more praise before wrapping up with a proclamation of peace and God's mercy on everyone.

In some parts of Africa, prayer involves rituals, dancing, chanting, music, dance, and sacrifices in honor of divine beings who bless the people benevolently for their devotion. How about Eastern religions? Mantras are commonplace in Hinduism and Buddhism. However, Buddhists do not subscribe to the idea of praying to a God or Goddess. Hinduism has a philosophical prayer and meditation on the essence of specific deities.

If you want to pray, there's one thing to always remember: Your intention matters. It's much better to make your prayer as personal as possible because it will be much more sincere and less rote than praying standard prayers (unless you pray those traditional prayers with a deep focus on their meanings).

Three Forms of Prayer

Conscious Intentional Prayer: This prayer requires you to focus your mind on attaining a specific result, your intention. You need a mental picture of the fulfillment of whatever you desire. Then, you leave it for the source of all life to handle, trusting that it will take care of it at the right time, not a moment too soon or too late, and in the best way for all concerned. Intention is the engine that drives your prayer forward until it becomes a fleshed-out result for everyone to see. It's the reason you get out of bed to pursue your dreams, smash your goals, and bring your desires to pass.

By incorporating the energy of intention into your prayers, you will be clear on what you hope to receive. It focuses your energy, making you more likely to receive what you want.

Conscious, intentional prayer requires a deliberate refocusing of your mind on your objective while you pray, holding your thoughts and emotions hostage to the end of your prayer time and disciplining them so they do not stray. What you assume and how you feel as you pray must match how you'd feel if you had the answer to your prayer already. This way, you put yourself in the best position for the Divine to help you. Your actions and choices will naturally be aligned with what you desire, and it's only a matter of time before you make your dream happen.

You can find this intentionality in the *Sankalpa* of Hinduism, a solemn vow, an intention you must make before you make your dreams happen. By being deliberate in offering your Sankalpa to the Universe, keeping your focus on the end goal already being real here and now, and staying devoted to that vision, you gather energy from every plane of existence and carve your world into the exact vision you want to see.

Conscious Awareness Prayer: Conscious awareness prayer is about remaining aware of how you're being and what you're thinking from moment to moment and ensuring it aligns with the essence of God. You have to be focused when working with this prayer. But rather than seeking outcomes, you're more interested in your inner world. What are you feeling in your body? How about emotionally? What are the thoughts at the moment? Ask yourself these questions without judging yourself. You're not making a particular request because the only thing that matters is remaining firmly rooted in the present, where your past and future are nonexistent concepts. For all you know, you might as well have suddenly appeared on Earth right now.

What's the point of this prayer? You'll become more self-aware, which automatically puts you in touch with your intuition. As your desires appear during your day, you'll naturally be led toward the answers you seek. Thanks to your deeper connection with your intuition, you'll be directed to take the right actions, say the right things, and be at the right place at the right time. Conscious awareness prayer is about staying open, accepting whatever is and whatever comes afterward. One thing you'll notice with this form of worship is that it's almost like meditation, in the sense that the ongoing monologue in your head is forced to shut up, giving you peace on the inside regardless of what's happening around you. You'll receive phenomenal, life-changing insights that will change your life for the better from this state. If you practice this prayer, you won't have to pray for specific things because things line up beautifully for you.

Unconscious Awareness Prayer: With this form of prayer, there's a connection between your specific intentions and awareness of your life experience in the here and now. In other words, it's the balance between conscious intention and conscious awareness. Not only do you have moments where you focus on your intention, but you ensure you're acting as someone who already has what they seek. Even when you're confronted with the evidence of the absence of your desire in the physical, you don't allow that to phase you. You continue to fix your mind on your fully fleshed-out manifestation (in your imagination) while tracking your experience of life, ensuring your mental chatter, emotions, actions, and vision match your desired reality.

Now you understand the basic mechanics of prayer- Remember, it's not just about honoring a deity because that's what you've been taught. It's a sincere act, one you do willingly. Prayer is a profound way to cultivate presence and mindfulness. The more you pray, the more you'll experience higher consciousness.

Practical Tips for Consistent, Meaningful Prayer

1. Don't use rituals if you're not comfortable. You don't need to use specific words from set prayers if they do not resonate, nor do you need to craft yours and repeat it until it loses meaning. You can simply become aware of the moment and set your intention before you begin.

2. Find a way to fit prayer into your routine to stay consistent. You could make prayer the last thing you do at night and the first thing you do before you get out of bed in the morning. You could take advantage of your lunch breaks, the moment before you enter your office building, or before you set off for home. It's up to you.
3. Don't just ask. Receive as well. How? When you are done asking, remain seated in silence and expect an answer. Note that it may not be in words. It could be a simple feeling of completion, certainty, satisfaction, ease, or something else.
4. Journal whatever you receive from prayer. This record will show you that it indeed works and help you through times when you waver in doubt.
5. Do not beat yourself up for skipping a day or two of prayer. At the same time, understand that you'll need time to establish consistency, so be kinder to yourself.

Chapter 10: A Continual Spiral of Growth

In this final chapter, you should remember that you are a part of the Divine Feminine. You are inseparable from her grace, mercy, and love. You carry her power and essence within you.

You are a part of the Divine Feminine.[39]

Celebrating Your Inner Goddess

As you develop your relationship with the Divine Feminine, you need to celebrate yourself. You must acknowledge how far you've come because it's no mean feat that you decided to pursue this path and followed through on your decision even though the world is a place where the toxic masculine attempts to smother the Divine Feminine in everyone. You have chosen the path less trodden, and as a result, you've become one of many who will eventually help the world break free from the imbalance of energies it's currently suffering.

Embracing your inner Goddess is not easy because it means overcoming the tendencies you've instilled in you since birth. It is a course of action that requires unlearning, and it is brutal. You have to chip away at the things you once thought of as part of your original self, realizing that they're simply ideas from others you accepted as your identity. There are times on this journey when it feels so painful and downright impossible to progress. So, if you've chosen to persevere and push through, you should definitely celebrate the courage and progress you've made so far.

It isn't easy to convince yourself that there are better ways than working yourself to the bone to accomplish abundance. Like others in the past, your default response to the idea of not needing to work hard to accomplish abundance would have been to scoff and laugh at its seeming ridiculousness. However, you have dared to prove this truth to yourself, which is not easy in the face of the very persistent illusion of needing to work yourself into the ground before accomplishing abundance.

There may have been times when life appeared to mock you. There may have been moments when you wondered if you weren't being silly or ridiculous, trying out this "Divine Feminine thing," wondering if it wouldn't be better to return to the status quo you were used to and familiar with. However, you've somehow found the courage to keep going. Your willingness, perseverance, and faith have rewarded you with evidence of new, better ways to achieve your dreams in life. It is something worth celebrating.

As you continue incorporating the Divine Feminine energy into your life, recognize that you will not always maintain a fixed level of this energy. You are not a static being. No one is. Everyone is designed to continue evolving, to fluctuate with respect to the dynamics of the Divine pendulum swinging from one energy to another. Therefore, if you find yourself out of balance, the last thing you should do is beat yourself up. Instead, be glad that you now have the consciousness to be aware of this shift in balance and do what you must return to your center.

It serves no one to feel terrible about being imperfect or flawed. The very nature of imperfection is a perfect design in nature. It is a feature, not a flaw, so don't dwell on your mistakes. See yourself as a work of art constantly, eternally in progress, ever evolving into something more refined. This way, rather than harshly criticize yourself, you can celebrate how far you've come from who you used to be to who you are now. You'll be excited about the prospect of who you'll morph into along your journey of embracing the Divine Feminine within.

Nurture Your

Your intuition will guide you further along the path to meeting your most balanced self.[80]

One of the most essential things to recall is constantly staying in touch with your intuition. It is your intuition that will guide you further and further along the path to meeting your most balanced self. Your intuition is that soft, still voice that will let you know when you're deviating from your goals. Whatever you do, honor it without question. At this point, you should have discovered the futility of attempting to interpret intuition using logic and rationality. It is much better to embrace it without question and discover later why it was essential to heed that voice warning and steering you this way and that.

Your ego seduces you into returning to the trap of logic. Remember, the idea behind logic is rooted in that which is familiar and already known. How can you possibly grow if you remain in the spaces you already know? How could you discover new lands if you only stay at home? How do you become more than you are if you insist on remaining exactly as you are?

Yet logic insists that you keep everything the same. Logic is ego-driven because your ego fears that if you dare to explore the unfamiliar, you may put yourself at risk, and it will no longer exist. The one thing the ego fears above everything else is nonexistence. So, it's essential to break away from the habits of the ego, to shun the tendency to retreat into the safety of logic and reason, and instead realize your existence can't be permanently extinguished or erased. Why? Because you are a soul, first and foremost, before a human being. You are an eternal being, one that can't be destroyed.

You may look around and see disease and death claiming people's lives. However, rest assured that those souls continue their next adventure in another reincarnation. Right now, you are a soul having a human adventure. Your ego doesn't understand it because it's terrified that this is all there is to life. It continues to do what it must to shield you. In its misguided opinion, it is keeping you safe from harm.

If there's one thing your ego knows about your intuition, it's that it will lead you into depths that it cannot fathom, where it suspects it will be destroyed. In a sense, this is true. As you practice expressing the energy of the Divine Feminine in your life, you will naturally be connected to higher consciousness and realize that the ego is a tool you can put down and pick up as needed. You'll learn that everything connected to your ego —who you are, what you like and dislike, your name, how much you make, what you do, etc. — is nothing but a mask or a costume. It's like putting on clothes and assuming they are who you are instead of knowing you can take them off your body and put on different ones. You can burn the clothes and still be perfectly fine.

So, if you are ever led to participate in a random conversation, even though it's not in your nature to interrupt others when speaking, you should. If you're not an avid reader but suddenly have the urge to read a specific book, listen to your intuition. If you've gone your entire life hating the idea of mathematics and numbers and yet suddenly want to learn about business bookkeeping or accounting, listen to your gut and follow through. If you've always assumed that you could never create anything close to the beautiful works of art you have seen from painters, sculptors, and other artists, but you suddenly are bitten by the art bug, follow that impulse and see where it goes.

In other words, be like a child. Have you ever watched little children when they play? If you take a toy away from them, they immediately pivot to the next shiny, interesting object. They don't pause to consider whether they want to play with that thing or not. They simply follow their little hearts. Unfortunately, over time, society dulls the instinct to follow your intuition and emphasizes the need to exercise caution and be logical, rational, and restrained in affairs of the heart.

Well, dear reader, it is time for you to throw that book out. It is time to return to being your inner child. Allow your intuition to lead you. Trust that it will always take you to beautiful places and watch the magic unfolding in your life. If you genuinely want to walk the path of the Divine Feminine, you don't have a choice in this matter, for it is through your intuition that her energy and wisdom flow and express themselves in your life. Through your intuition, your spirit guides will lead you where you must go to experience the next best version of yourself. By following your intuition, you offer a gift to others, showing them the path to healing and reflecting on the possibilities they could enjoy.

Conclusion

You can no longer afford to play small. You can't afford to keep doing things the way you've always have. Having read this book, you've answered the Divine Feminine's call, and now her fire rages within you, demanding attention. Should you choose to disregard the information you've learned from these pages, you'll find that the costumes and masks you continue to insist on wearing will become heavier than ever. Trust this one fact: You do not want the heaviness to progress past a certain point. The burden of answering the Divine Feminine's call is much lighter than insisting on maintaining the charade of the life you've lived so far. She's offering you something far better than you can imagine. There's only one way to receive it: to dare to step into the unknown.

It is time to burn the bridge that still connects you to all that you hold familiar and dear. It's time to step into new territory to discover what more lies within you. You carry greatness, strength, resilience, courage, love, light, abundance, and many other gifts only you can discover by daring to take the Divine Feminine's hand. Allow her to show you the way to your authentic self. You deserve to live the life you've always dreamed of. For the longest time, you've always suspected that things could be better than they are, and you are right. You now know how to achieve this better life you've always wanted. It would be a crying shame if you denied yourself the gift of fulfilling your dreams.

Do you feel terrified? Are you being dogged by uncertainty and fear? This is perfectly normal. It is to be expected. However, you must demonstrate courage. It does not mean you will not be afraid. It means you will acknowledge your fear and still act despite it. It is a sad state of affairs that society has taught everyone to be afraid of being afraid. There is a reason for this and it is an insidious one. Here's a good rule of thumb for you to live by going forward: If something terrifies you or makes you afraid, that is exactly what you should chase after. Your fears give you clues about what you should be doing with your life. So, if the thought of embracing the Divine Feminine and finding your inner Goddess terrifies you, you know what to do. It is your one task; you must see it through to the end and beyond. The fear you feel may tell you that you aren't ready. But that is a big lie.

Remember, there are no coincidences. There's only one reason you and this book have found each other: you are ready *now*. You're as prepared as you'll ever be. So, take the plunge and see what's on the other side. Beware, though, you will never be the same again, but it'll be for the better.

You're never alone. Remember that. You are the Divine Mother's own.

Part 2: Sacred Masculine Energy

Unlocking Your Inner Strength and Connecting with the Divine Masculine to Achieve Clarity, Focus, and Balance

Introduction

The sacred masculine is the energy of action. There is a huge misconception about the divine feminine and divine masculine that constricts these vast expanses of existence to gender identity. Therefore, it is crucial to understand that the sacred masculine and feminine are the personification of timeless observations about the functioning of reality and the human condition. Everything in existence is on a spectrum. The opposite ends of some of these spectrums are labeled masculine and feminine for people to better understand the universe in a palatable and consumable way. Human beings express themselves and organize their societies according to their needs and biology. Although cultures vastly differ, some common understandings and behaviors are embedded deep into people's evolutionary history.

These expressions of humanity have been understood in different ways throughout the ages. Some use religion and spirituality, and in modern times, science and psychology are the lenses applied to these observations. Regardless of how you look at it, fundamental truths will be revealed when you begin to analyze these common threads. One of the most fundamental of these many truths is that consciousness and matter work together to manifest the reality in which people find themselves. Everything begins with a thought. Before a man and woman come together to make a baby, their relationship begins in the mind through attraction. This attraction is then acted upon through their behaviors, and if both people are on board, a child is made.

The thoughts that were the progenitor of the behavior are abstract and intangible, but the actions are more defined. This abstractness can be perceived as the divine feminine, while the solid and more tangible actions are the sacred masculine. This book will explore the inner work you can do, be it spiritual or psychological, so that the channel of masculine energy can be guided in a way most beneficial to you, those around you, and society.

Understanding the science of archetypes and narrative formation and diving into meditation and mindfulness practices will unlock the sacred masculine within you to its fullest extent. Everyone has a dream or vision within them. This book will teach you how to condense that vision into the external world from the abstract space through the masculine portals of discipline, self-control, rationality, focus, perseverance, courage, resilience, and strength.

By conscientiously applying the sciences of the divine masculine, you can take action to transform the world into your image. There is a huge responsibility to embody the role of the divine masculine because suffering and perseverance are part of the journey. This book prepares you for the hurdles you'll face when pursuing your dreams and desires while giving you the tools to mold life according to your imagination and internal reality.

Chapter 1: What Is the Sacred Masculine?

To understand masculine energy, you must first contrast it with feminine energy. Masculine and feminine on an energetic level fall into two Hermetic principles: the principle of gender and the principle of polarity. The principle of polarity means that everything within existence and its opposite are the same things being expressed in different ways. For example, hot or cold are both an expression of temperature and, therefore, are one. In essence, masculine and feminine are one expression of opposite polarities. This means that both masculine and feminine energy are the same in certain ways. The principle of gender is more closely related to masculinity and femininity because it outlines how everything within the universe has a feminine and a masculine expression.

Masculine and feminine are an expression of opposite polarities.[81]

It is easy to think that the sacred masculine means men and the divine feminine means women. However, this is a common misconception. If you limit your focus to humans, it becomes clear that men and women both contain masculine and feminine energy. At the biological level, half of your DNA comes from your father, and the other half comes from your mother. Both masculine and feminine are present for you to exist regardless of your outward biological expression. So, if feminine and masculine cannot simply be boxed into men and women, you may ask: what do these energies represent?

Unpacking the divine masculine requires you to first break down the words "feminine" and "masculine." When you analyze the word "masculine," you find that the last part of the word is "line." This hints at what masculine energy is. A line moves straight forward and goes directly from point A to point B. Contrast this with the word "feminine," and you'll find that the end of the word is "nine." Think of the number 9. Nine has a curve. Feminine energy is not as straightforward as the masculine. It works in waves, representing the more abstract part of the human identity.

Once you grasp that the masculine represents a line and a direct approach, its details can be further understood. The sacred masculine is all about taking action. The feminine is the internal work, while the masculine is the external. If you look at it through the lens of traditional gender roles, a clearer picture can be painted. In the past, women were expected to stay inside the house, while men were expected to go out and work for their families. Now, understand that this is not a promotion of traditional gender roles but rather a symbolic representation of how masculine and feminine energy function. Think of the home as your internal environment and the work that men go out to do as your external environment. Your emotions, thoughts, and beliefs that inform your actions are the feminine, while your expressions of your thoughts, emotions, and beliefs are the masculine.

The sacred masculine can then be broken down into how you engage with society. The divine feminine is the womb, while the divine masculine is the child. The child has to get pushed out of the womb to engage with the external reality once it is ready. Therefore, the sacred masculine is the mark you leave on the world. Another societal expression that makes masculine energy clearer is the tradition of a couple getting married and the wife taking their husband's name. The legacy of the external world comes through the paternal line or lineage. Take note of the words "line" or "lineage" as it relates to "masculine."

So, in a nutshell, the sacred masculine is about the imprint you leave or the expression of yourself to the outside world. The masculine is what you show, while the feminine is what you keep hidden. Another way to think about it is feminine is the darkness, and masculinity is the light. Light and dark in this context have nothing to do with good and evil. The light is revealing, while the darkness is all-consuming.

Qualities of the Divine Masculine

The divine masculine drive to action will be expressed in various ways. One of the primary ways that the divine masculine is manifested is through order, as opposed to feminine chaos. Too much order is terrible, just like an excess of chaos is detrimental. The key is to find a balance between your sacred masculine and feminine energies. Order is about rules, regulations, and discipline, while chaos is about free-flowing expression. Your divine masculine qualities will be expressed within a set framework: religious rules, political ideology, an ethical system, or the corporate world.

When you examine masculine qualities, attributes, and expressions, you find that they are all based on instituting or defending a principle or code. For example, strength is one of the first masculine qualities that pop into most people's minds. You are either going to use strength to build or to defend. The same is true for other masculine qualities like leadership, focus, assertiveness, and courage. Using your sacred masculinity to manifest the reality you want is not about these attributes or characteristics themselves but rather what vision you have that you are using these attributes to implement. For masculinity to be fully expressed, the feminine must be presented. Since the feminine exists in the abstract, your hopes and dreams can be classed under the divine feminine. However, for these dreams to grow out of the feminine womb, a seed must be planted, and this is where focus, leadership, courage, and assertiveness enter the picture.

The sacred masculine ensures that your vision does not remain in the void or the "womb." The divine masculine is meant to take on strain. When you neglect your masculine energy, your visions never come to fruition because you don't go out and get them. Overthinking is the main blockage to the manifestation of masculine energy. The most successful people in the world don't spend too much time thinking, but they do what needs to be done. Your fear can hold you back as you dance in the chaos of made-up scenarios. Using your sacred masculine means taking action and figuring things out with resilience and problem-solving. The masculine mind is analytical, so it is what orders the chaos of creativity. Think of creativity, which is required for your dreams and visions, as a wild horse. This horse is powerful and runs wild and free. Your analytical masculine energy comes in to tame and set it on a direct path or in a straight line. Masculine energy transmutes the abstract into the concrete.

The Misinterpreted Masculine

The misinterpreted masculine is what is typically referred to as *toxic masculinity*. This is when your masculine energy is out of balance with the feminine, so it spills over into a domineering and oppressive space. Misogyny and patriarchy are the consequences of imbalanced masculine energy.

The misinterpreted masculine comes from insecurity, *which is far from masculinity*. In some men, insecurity causes them to freeze up and not move to do what is needed. In others, it causes an imbalanced overcompensation, which gets expressed aggressively through the attempt to control – instead of *leading* others.

For example, a blue-collar worker may experience extreme exploitation and oppression at his job. As a result, he suppresses his masculine essence in order to assert himself and stamp his mark on the world – creating a feeling of lack. Due to this lack, he may go home and feel the need to overexert his power because his house is where he has some say in a world that suppresses him. This can then result in emotional, physical, and psychological abuse. The tyranny that he experiences in the exploitation, which is also caused by the misinterpreted masculine of wanting more without end, will then take root in his home, creating a chain reaction of oppression. The man may have a son who will now exert oppressive power over those that he can, like abusing a pet or bullying other children at school. The misinterpreted masculine is like a social rot or disease that infects everything it comes into contact with.

In a materialistic world with stereotypes, freedom from these chains is necessary.[82]

In a world where misogyny, patriarchy, oppression, and tyranny run rife, a masculine revolution is needed. Envisioning a world free from these poisons is not enough. The divine masculine has to propel you to take action. The divine masculine has righteous and wicked expressions. When this energy is tainted, it aims to oppress and control *instead of uplift and guide*. The misinterpreted masculine is a slave driver whipping people from behind to do his bidding.

In contrast, the actualized masculine is the one that leads their people from the front into a brighter future by being the example. The divine masculine has the perfect balance of competitiveness and cooperation instead of the misinterpreted masculine that wants to win at all costs, even to the detriment of others, including their team. The only way to be free from the distorted masculine is to grow from the healed feminine space of compassion, nurturing, and emotional intelligence.

Historical and Mythological Roots of the Divine Masculine

The divine masculine goes back to the beginning of time. The Genesis creation account in the Bible describes the earth in the beginning as formless and void. This is representative of the womb of creation. You can also look at it more scientifically when physicists describe the universe coming from nothing. Nothing can be represented as the womb. The formless void must be ordered through the masculine filter to create something. This is where the Biblical God, often personified as male, begins to take action and order creation with his words. These words represent a vibration or a movement to implement the change you want to see, which, in essence, is the basis of the divine masculine. Similar myths of the order coming out of the chaotic primordial waters are contained throughout various cultures' creation myths.

In mythology and fiction, the divine masculine typically manifests as one of four archetypes (or some combination of them). These archetypes are the **king, lover, magician, and warrior**.

The **king** represents leadership and overcoming hardships. The archetype of the king is trialed, and once he prevails, he earns his right to rule. He is primal and deals with order, honor, and virtue.

The **warrior** represents the destructive capacity of the divine masculine in mythology. However, the warrior's violence is to bring forth the greater good. He has an ideological background like a knight, so he is not consumed by mindless savagery.

A **magician** usually guides the king or warrior. The magician is the knowledge or expert expression of the divine masculine that takes a secondary position of support. He is extremely powerful, but he uses his power to uplift others.

Lastly, you have the **lover** archetype, which is about pleasure and worldly desires. The lover expression is needed in the divine masculine because stamping yourself on a world that you hate and gain no pleasure from results in destruction.

You see these archetypes being repeated in different stories, myths, and legends throughout the globe.

In the primal state, masculine and feminine energy were more closely aligned to their physical or biological expression, although there have been overlaps since the beginning. Asexual reproduction evolved before sexual reproduction. Somewhere in humanity's distant past – before people became human – they were unicellular organisms, so the masculine and feminine were more explicitly embodied in one being. The key concept of evolution is *survival of the fittest*, which, unlike many people, misunderstand it to mean it is not about force or strength. Survival of the fittest means those most adjusted or suited to an environment will thrive.

For whatever reason, nature chose to develop sexual reproduction to institute genetic diversity and make offspring more resilient to environmental changes. Therefore, humanity's oldest ancestors had male in female and female in male.

However, at some point when sexual reproduction and gender developed, nature called for more solidified roles for each sex. These roles carried into how societies were built and evolved with time according to the needs of mankind. The world has progressed so much that these gaps are closing. For example, the necessity for men to protect women is lower than it once was because of technological development and women being able to protect themselves better. The same is true for provision because women are also now in the workplace. It is becoming more apparent that either sex can embody masculine and feminine energy.

The next level of human expression is finding the balance that has been recorded in trinitarian mythologies of the mother, father, and child (like Auset, Ausar, and Heru in the Egyptian pantheon, or Shiva, Parvati, and Ganesha in the Hindu pantheon). All three are embodied within all people, and to be fully actualized, you must understand all of these expressions. This book only focuses on the divine masculine, though.

Male Identity Crisis

In the past, it was clear what was expected of a man. Feminist movements and the progressive shifting of societal attitudes coupled with accelerated technological development have placed women in spaces they have never been in before. These changes have disturbed the masculine energy within males because masculinity wants what is clear and defined, and in the modern context, the lines have become blurred. In past times, men protected and provided while women nurtured and cared for the home and family. These structures are no longer so clear-cut, especially in trying economic times where most households need dual incomes to stay afloat. This progress has unwittingly caused a crisis of masculinity where too many men have no idea how they fit into the societal structure. Unfortunately, it has also caused many toxic ideas and influencers to rise, especially in the online space with "alpha male podcasts" and the "Red Pill" community.

This redefining of masculinity for men does not have to be a crisis but can be transitioned into an opportunity. There is still so much wrong with the world and problems that need to be solved, which is where masculine energy works its magic. For a man to stand strong in the fullness of his masculinity, he has to do some introspective soul-searching to find out what he wants to be, how he relates to the world, and what mark he wants to leave on the planet. Once these questions are answered, a man can channel his masculinity to take focused action and confidently assert himself to shape the world and, more importantly, himself in the image of his vision. There is no longer a cookie-cutter mold of what it means to be a man, so there is freedom for you to bravely carve out a path into the unknown and stake a claim in the new world that society is creating together.

Where men were once given a masculine identity, it is now the time to create one. You don't need to listen to bald men shouting into a podcast microphone, trying to sell you overpriced scam courses about what you need to do to be a man! Sacred masculinity is about leading the way forward – but before you can lead others, you must guide yourself. Start with the mirror, then expand into your home, and then your community and build from there. The divine masculine is what gives you the power to shape the world like the people before you who instituted the roles that are now breaking down. Your mold of masculinity is decentralized, which puts a lot more of the power and responsibility in your hands to determine how you are going to manifest your masculinity.

The Fluidity of Gender and Inclusivity

There have been matriarchal and patriarchal societies depending on the time and region you find yourself in. Now, the world is entering a space of balance. The reorganization required to find this balance has questioned gender identities and how they have been understood, particularly in a Westernized context. Many are resisting this question. However, the ball is already rolling. How people understand sex, gender, and gender roles is rapidly shifting. This is the feminine period of chaos before the masculine period of order comes into play, so society is still navigating the unknown regarding gender identity and how people want to define themselves. Eventually, a natural equilibrium will be reached, but it will be way different than what the world has been conditioned to accept.

Sex and gender identity have become two separate concepts. One does not have to express the gender that aligns with their sex anymore. This shows that masculine and feminine are spiritual concepts that operate in the realm of energy that are only tangentially tied to biology. It is easy to box these concepts into man and woman when speaking of divine feminine and sacred masculine. People often think of it as women should exhibit the sacred feminine and men should exhibit the sacred masculine without understanding how limiting this view is. All genders embody the divine masculine because everyone needs to take action and move analytically at different moments in life. When you look at temperament, typically, men show masculine qualities more often than women, but no woman is free from masculine energy on a spiritual or biological level *because the seed and the soil are both needed to bring forth life.*

This book will highlight the psychological, biological, and spiritual overlaps, but the sacred masculine will be explored predominantly on an energetic and vibratory level. Your gender identity is irrelevant to whether you can embody the sacred masculine because that aspect is a part of all humans. As you dive deeper into the sacred masculine and understand how embracing it can benefit your life, you'll begin to realize that it is not your gender that drives you but your energy that gets condensed into the physical. By taking analytical action through the sacred masculine, you can construct your reality from the ground up by balancing the unseen and the seen in ways that will profoundly change your life.

Chapter 2: The Archetypes

Archetypes: The Jungian Connection

Carl Jung is considered by many to be one of the fathers of modern psychology. However, his work continued beyond the realm of psychology or how people would conceptualize it today. Jung explored mythologies and story structures as they relate to the development of mankind. From this study came the concept of archetypes. Jung described archetypes as common patterns and symbols that emerged from the collective unconscious of humanity. Because of this, you'll find similar story structures across cultures and times that get repeated as if they are embodied deep within the DNA of humanity.

Jung explored mythologies and story structures as they relate to the development of mankind.[38]

Jung theorized that the collective identity functions at a lower form of consciousness than the individual. You then find phenomena like mob mentality, where people in a group do horrific things that they could never do alone. These tropes, or archetypes, are almost automatic and are probably sown deep into people's genetic past and evolutionary history. Studying these archetypes reveals deeply hidden driving forces that guide individual actions and how society is structured. In the light of the sacred masculine, which is driven by focused action, these archetypes show up in a variety of ways, both beneficial and detrimental. It can be enlightening to explore how archetypes present themselves in fiction and mythology and how they manifest in daily life. You will then be able to assess which archetypes you align with at different periods in your life so you can make informed decisions about how to maximize the greatness of the tropes you embody and integrate the shadow of these archetypes to turn negativity into positivity.

The Hero's Journey

The hero's journey is one of the two-story structures that every written work or oral tradition follows. An impactful narrative will either be a hero's journey or a tragedy. Tragedies are stories of the downfall of the capable and usually include how misdirected ambition can cause destruction. Tragedy is common in Shakespearean works like Macbeth or Othello. The hero's journey is something that most people get introduced to as children.

The hero story structure begins with the protagonist in his ordinary world, which then gets disrupted for some reason. He then gets a call to action to address this disruption. The hero will undergo some training and will inevitably fail at first. This failure will cause the hero to fight battles internally and address their shortcomings before returning to defeat the antagonist and restore order. Once the villain is defeated, equilibrium is reinstated, but the world and the hero are forever changed. This structure can be applied to many battles that people face in their lives. The beginning of the hero's journey is the call to action, equating to the activation of the divine masculine that begins unfolding as the narrative progresses.

The Symbology of Archetypes and Their Relevance in Your Life

In the Jungian understanding, there are four main archetypes: the ***persona***, the ***shadow***, the ***anima*** (or animus), and the ***self***. From these four archetypes emerge the archetypal figures, which manifest themselves through narrative structures.

The *persona* is the mask you wear before the world.

The *shadow* is the parts of yourself that are repressed, yet they motivate many of your actions.

The *anima* is the feminine projection in the male mind, while the *animus* is the male projection in the female psyche.

The *self* is the combination of the conscious and unconscious of an individual. These four archetypes give rise to 12 archetypal figures embodied in real-world behavior and are used to tell stories. By exploring these archetypal figures, you can begin mapping yourself in relation to the world by expressing your masculine energy.

Each of these archetypal figures can be categorized into ego, order, social, and freedom. The ego is concerned with making your presence felt or obtaining some form of validation and admiration. Order is all about maintaining and establishing social structures. Social aims to build bonds with others – and freedom – is about overcoming physical and psychological limitations. The archetypal figures will have one of these categories as their primary motivation.

It is important to remember that you will not fall *neatly* into any of these archetypes; you'll most likely express many of them in your multifaceted life, even if one emerges as a primary identifier of your behavior. You may embody one archetype at home, another at work, and a different one in social settings. The archetype you most relate to may change with time and as you learn. Therefore, don't get too caught up with trying to identify with one archetypal figure, but rather see how all of them show up in your life to gain a deeper insight into your motivations so that you can use the divine masculine within you to direct your actions through the filter of these figures. These archetypal figures are not you but rather a map to navigate the infinite complexity of the human being.

The Innocent

This archetypal figure represents naivety and is an over-trusting individual. You may see this in films as someone who was sheltered or comes from a completely different world learning to exist in a new space. The innocent overlook threats and live in delusion due to their ignorance. They are pure of heart, and their negativity is not malicious but rather a result of their child-like misunderstanding. In fiction, you can think of Alice in Wonderland or Dorothy from The Wizard of Oz, who unwittingly fall into all types of dangerous and adventurous situations.

This archetypal figure represents naivety, like Alice from Alice in Wonderland, who unwittingly falls into all types of dangerous and adventurous situations.⁸⁴

The shadow of the innocent is a complete denial of reality. That manifests as an over-optimistic outlook on life and can often be a burden to those around them who have to clean up the messes they make. The innocent is the embodiment of unfiltered righteousness. Due to their naivety, the innocent is easy to take advantage of. Forrest Gump is the perfect fictional representation of the innocent because his simple and pure worldview misses much of the darkness that occurs in the film. The shadow of the innocent can also show up as addiction or perpetual childhood due to being unable to accept reality at face value.

The tainting of the innocent is reflected in the often-told story of a child star that spirals. They enter the daprk environment of Hollywood without the tools to see exploitation. This process can be seen with the spiraling of stars like Justin Bieber, Lindsey Lohan, and Britney Spears. Integration of the shadow means bringing unconscious motivations into the conscious or shining light into the darkness. Taking masculine action to integrate the shadow of the innocent means keeping a playful spirit while becoming more aware of the danger of ascending from a child-like state. For example, a musician may keep an innocent and playful nature to make good music, but they should also study the industry's business side to prevent themselves from getting exploited.

The Everyman

The everyman is precisely what the name describes. This individual is the ultimate average and simply wants to fit into the role that society has carved out. In fiction, this is usually the character that is inserted for the audience to relate to. In Scott F. Fitzgerald's Great Gatsby, Nick Carraway is a perfect example of an average character who gets thrown into the middle of the extraordinary world of Jay Gatsby to act as the reader's eyes. In the context of the novel, Nick Carraway is seeking to fit into the world of the rich and famous that Jay introduces him to.

In their attempt to fit in, the everyman usually sticks out like a sore thumb. Their need to be accepted often gets them taken advantage of. Integrating the everyman shadow requires you to internally seek out the motivation for your desire to fit in. From there, you can make more informed decisions about what you will conform to. Another downside of this archetype is getting absorbed into the background. The masculine energy of assertiveness is needed to break the shell of the everyman and leave your imprint in any room you enter.

Nick Carraway is a perfect example of an average character who gets thrown into the middle of an extraordinary world.[55]

The Hero

Justice is the primary motivator of the hero archetype. The hero fights for what they view as right and, along their journey, has to evolve to bring forth this perceived good into the world. The shadow of the hero is the tunnel vision that creates blinders blocking out every perspective of morality other than their own. When manifested in the dark side, the hero can get so consumed by their idealistic view that they become villains. If you take the Hermetic principle of polarity to analyze a hero, you realize that heroes and villains exist on the same spectrum. Someone may feel that their cause is just, but the outcomes of their actions will overshadow their intentions.

The hero is one of the most common archetypes in storytelling, which is why the hero's journey is such a repeated narrative arch. An example of a hero in mythology is Heru from the Egyptian pantheon, which is the linguistic root of the word "hero." Heru fights Set for the Earthly throne that was usurped from his father, Ausar. Heru has to come out of hiding to face his father's murder. This is an amazing embodiment of the divine masculine principle because it shows how you need to come out of the darkness to face your battles. That darkness may be the idea in your mind that you have not followed through on literal isolation. The hero has to accept the call to action, which is the activation of masculine energy.

The Outlaw/Rebel

Robin Hood is one of modern culture's most popular outlaw or rebel embodiments. He rebels against the system and steals from the rich to give to the poor. The outlaw, much like the hero, is driven by idealism. However, instead of functioning within the boundaries that have been set out for them, they reject all the institutions they view as corrupt. The hero and outlaw duality is like Superman and The Punisher. Superman has strict moral guidelines that would appease the sensibilities of the broader systems, while The Punisher takes morally ambiguous actions to achieve his goals. Their intentions are similar, but their methods are entirely different.

A modern-day example of the outlaw archetype is "hacktivists." These individuals illegally hack into various systems to achieve a perceived positive political or social goal. A popular group of hacktivists is Anonymous. One of their actions was against PayPal, Visa, and MasterCard after they refused to work with WikiLeaks, who were leaking governmental

A modern-day example of the outlaw archetype is a hacktivist.[86]

documents showing corruption. The hackers crashed the sites because of their actions against the whistleblower platform. The shadow of the outlaw is a nihilistic outlook of all systems and a rejection of reform from within. Integrating the rebel archetype means becoming open to working with people with similar goals within the institutions they reject. The outlaw archetype is one of the bravest expressions of masculine energy because it means taking action against the norms of the society you function within, inspired by a moral code.

The Explorer

The explorer archetype is a more self-centered expression of masculinity. The explorer is driven by adventure and independence, always looking to pave a new way. The mantra of self-determination consumes this archetype. The explorer archetype has been popularized in films like Indiana Jones. An explorer faces danger purely for the thrill of it. The shadow of the explorer is instability and the urge to always be on the move. It is challenging to build on such unstable ground. In reality, the explorer archetype appears in many ways, like someone who is constantly job-hopping or people who constantly travel, like the new modern emergence of digital nomads taking online jobs so they don't feel tied down. It can be difficult to establish strong relationships as an explorer. Therefore, integrating the shadow of the explorer requires grounding and connections to some form of stability.

The explorer is driven by adventure and independence.[87]

The Creator

When you think of the creator archetype, think of artists, musicians, innovators, inventors, and everyone who brings forth something new into the world. The creator archetype, as the name suggests, must create. In fiction, one of the most popular characters that express the creator archetype is Tony Stark, Iron Man from the Marvel movies and comics. Iron Man is a brilliant inventor who finds meaning in creation. The creator archetype expresses themselves through their creations. When their morality or ideology shifts, their creations will change along with it, like a songwriter whose lyrics evolve as they mature.

The creator archetype expresses themselves through their creations.[88]

The shadow of the creator is procrastination, self-doubt, fear of failure, and unfinished projects. Integration of the shadow for the creator archetype requires accepting that people may not love your work and embracing organizational skills to stick to set timelines. Fear and doubt are the killers of creativity. The sacred masculine is used to move beyond this paralyzing point of over-analysis and criticism to take action and create the work you feel called to.

The King

A king or a ruler's function is to instill order in a community or society. Since order and leadership are classed under masculine energy, this archetype facilitates a powerful connection to the sacred masculine. For the king archetype to be expressed healthily, there must be balance. Two shadows of the ruler can manifest negatively: the tyrant and the weakling. The tyrant is an authoritarian style of leadership where no one else gets a say and all freedom is suppressed, and the weakling is the pushover leader who gets swayed left and right because of outside pressure. The shadow of the king is integrated by finding a balance between taking suggestions and asserting himself.

A king or a ruler's function is to instill order in a community or society.[39]

The destructive aspects of the king archetype are elitism, being overly controlling, and an aversion to chaotic spontaneity. Being too immovable can be destructive, like a tree that is too rigid to bend with strong winds. The ruler archetype shows up in any leadership role, including a company CEO, a team captain or coach, or a political leader like a president or governor. In media, a healthy king archetype is Mufasa from The Lion King, who leads in a stern but fair way, only dealing out discipline when needed, taking advice from his servants, and giving praise where it is due.

The Magician

A magician walks a tightrope between the seen and unseen realms to transmute dreams into reality. You can consider the magician as the bridge between the abstract divine feminine and the rigid, analytical, sacred masculine. When the magician shows up in narratives, it is often a male with a flamboyant flair related to femininity. The magician represents the balance between the two. The magician is often in the role of the assistant to a hero, helping them transform into their full capacity. In the real world, the magician will, therefore, be someone taking on the position of a mentor, advisor, or right-hand man.

A magician walks a tightrope between the seen and unseen realms to transmute dreams into reality.[40]

The shadow of the magician is their tendency to be manipulative and deceptive. This is because they understand that reality is not grounded in facts and logic but rather in narrative and perspective, so they play with these views. The magician plays with these perceptions either to teach or just for fun. King Arthur's mentor, the wizard Merlin, is a brilliant depiction of the magician in fiction and mythology. One of the most famous people aligned with the magician archetype is the literal magic practitioner Aleister Crowley. The controversial Crowley is loved and hated by many. He reshaped how the occult is understood and instituted some of the most widely practiced forms of ceremonial magic. Crowley also embodied some of the downsides of the magician archetype with broken relationships, drug abuse, and excessive pleasure.

The Lover

Aphrodite, the goddess of love in the ancient Greek pantheon, is a perfect example of the lover archetype. This archetype is based on chasing pleasure and emotional highs. Aphrodite never settles down with just one partner, instead moving between multiple lovers. Aphrodite is a sexual partner for half the males on Olympus, but there are a few narratives that get highlighted more often. The purpose of the lover is to find fulfillment in relationships.

This archetype is based on chasing pleasure and emotional highs.[41]

The lover's shadow is the objectification of others and the inability to establish a lasting intimate bond. They are always looking for the next high or more intense emotional experience by zooming in on the flaws of their current relationships and idealizing their next partner. To integrate the shadow of the lover archetype and take masculine action, you need to decentralize your passion for romantic relationships and place that on some of your other goals. Falling in passionate love with various creative or business projects can help you channel the lover archetype to promote productivity instead of emotional turmoil and unfulfillment.

The Caregiver

Caregivers are motivated by altruism and often self-sacrifice. Their selfless generosity is dedicated to uplifting their loved ones or society and maximizing their well-being. A masculine representation of the caregiver is Denzel Washington's character, Robert McCall, in The Equalizer. He puts himself in danger to fight Russian mobsters to protect the female protagonist, Teri, whom he does not know. The caregiver's shadow is the feeling of inadequacy that they are not doing enough for others and neglect their well-being.

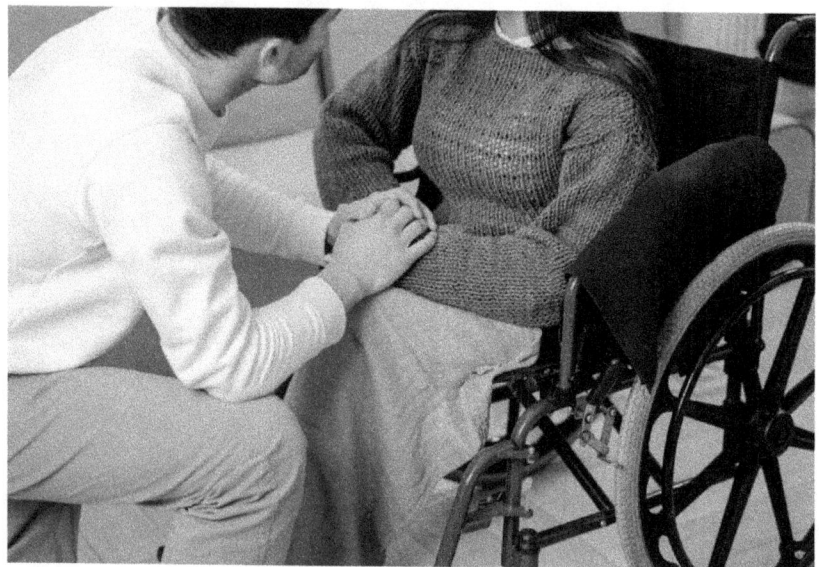

Caregivers are motivated by altruism and often self-sacrifice.⁴²

In everyday life, people who strongly embody caregivers are the ones that others run to when they are in need. They often get involved in charities and can sometimes be easily manipulated by a convincing sob story. You need to establish firm boundaries to integrate the shadow of self-neglect that the caregiver has. The caregiver must set rules for themselves for whom they are willing to help and what kind of behaviors should result in them withdrawing their help. Furthermore, self-care is an essential aspect of existing fully as a caregiver.

The Jester

Another name for the jester is the trickster. Trickster deities have been feared, hated, and revered throughout cultures. In the Yoruba tradition of West Africa, the trickster deity, Anansi, is a shapeshifter that often appears in the form of a spider. Anansi is known for playing tricks on people that sometimes have dire consequences to either teach them a lesson, to get what he wants, as well as for entertainment or vengeance. Jesters tend to live in the moment and enjoy life without overthinking the past or future. The shadow of the jester manifests in the rejection of responsibility, and they can also fall into addictive patterns. You've probably met someone who aligns with the jester archetype, or you may fit into the mold. Jesters never take anything seriously but are always fun to be around due to their jovial nature. To integrate the shadow, people who relate to the jester archetype need to stay away from substances and, more importantly, learn impulse control. Jesters can use their ability to look on the bright side of life and view things more light-heartedly as a tool to solve problems.

Jesters never take anything seriously but are always fun to be around due to their jovial nature.⁴⁸

The Sage

Knowledge and wisdom are the markers of the sage archetype. A popular sage in fiction is Morpheus from the film The Matrix. Morpheus teaches Neo all about the real world and breaks him free from the illusions he was trapped in to reach his full potential. The shadow of the sage archetype is the need to always be objective and the propensity to be judgmental. Sages, in reality, usually are mentors or religious leaders. In some ways, the sage is the pinnacle of the sacred masculine because they balance study to obtain knowledge with practical application to gain wisdom. However, their certainty can alienate some people and break helpful social bonds. To integrate the shadow of the sage archetype, they need to be more forgiving and open-minded to subjective viewpoints by occasionally listening to others instead of teaching.

Knowledge and wisdom are the markers of the sage archetype."

Chapter 3: Awakening Your Divine Masculine Energy

The divine masculine is in a deep slumber. Constraints and uncertainty have led to the suppression of this essential world-changing energy. Some forces want a docile population that is easier to control. Therefore, your self-determination and masculine compulsions deeply embedded in your genetics, psyche, and spirit are being suppressed. Much work needs to be done to unleash the sacred masculine from the bondage it has been subjected to. By understanding how archetypal figures relate to you, mindfulness, visualization, and practices to integrate your shadow, your sacred masculinity can be unleashed to propel you to heights you never thought possible.

The divine masculine can emerge from within through mindfulness.[45]

Identifying Your Dominant Archetype

Here are twelve questions. More than one may apply to you, but look within to see which one matches your personality the most. Ask yourself which of these you deeply resonate with, and it will help you determine your dominant archetype.

- **Are you ambitious, goal-orientated, and driven?**

  You are the hero archetype.

- **Are you orderly and organized?**

  You are the ruler archetype.

- **Do you love experiencing and discovering new things?**

  You are the explorer archetype.

- **Are you drawn to creative projects like art, music, or inventions?**

  You are the creator archetype.

- **Do you enthusiastically love people and get excited about new relationships?**

  You are the lover archetype.

- **Do you have a nurturing and caring nature?**

  You are the caregiver archetype.

- **Are you easy to relate to and get along with many different kinds of people?**

  You are the everyman archetype.

- **Do you often study, learn, and research, and people see you as wise?**

  You are the sage archetype.

- **Are you daring and rebellious, constantly questioning authority?**

  You are the outlaw archetype.

- **Are you drawn to healing and problem-solving?**

  You are the magician archetype.

- **Do you love to entertain people and often make jokes?**

  You are the jester archetype.

- **Do you follow the rules and strongly desire to fit in?**

  You are the innocent archetype.

Visualizations and Meditation

The first Hermetic principle is that all is mental. As the 17th-century French Philosopher Rene Descartes put it, "I think therefore I am." Your masculine transformation starts from within. Your mind does not control you because you are in charge of it. Yes, automatic actions occur in your mind, but you can tame them and direct them with sacred masculine order. Meditation and visualization are two of the most potent ways to begin reforming your mind. Now that you have identified your dominant archetype, you can implement meditations and practices that explicitly cater to your personality and temperament to attract the purest form of masculine energy and direct it to your benefit. Bear in mind that the exercises applied for each dominant archetype can be used by all people due to the multifaceted nature of humans. So, be open to trying various techniques regardless of which archetype fits you more closely.

The Outlaw

In its highest masculine expression, the outlaw takes action to overturn corrupt or unjust systems. For you to excel, you must visualize the world you want to create. Close your eyes in a quiet and safe space. Visualize the world you want to see. That does not necessarily have to be a grand global scheme. You can focus it on your household or community. Now, think about the institutions and actions you take that prevent this world you are visualizing from manifesting. Now, imagine how you can overcome and navigate the systems in the rebellious way that appeals to you and, most importantly, that brings you and society the most benefit.

The Magician

As someone who aligns with the magician archetype, you have an affinity for flair and theatrics. What is a magician without the explosions, the smoke and mirrors, or the showmanship? Your meditation as a magician aims to alchemize your reality from a space of imagination and enhance your guiding principle of wisdom. Your meditations as a magician can become more impactful with the use of rituals. Set up your space with candles, incense, colors, or whatever else you are intuitively drawn to. Candles are lovely meditation tools. Sit down with a candle in front of you. Control your breath and breathe in through your nose and out your mouth. Stare at the flame. When your mind wanders, bring your attention back to the flame and how the fire dances. After about 15 to 30 minutes of this, write down what first comes to mind. This gives you access to the hidden wisdom of your subconscious and will direct you where you can place the masculine energy of action.

The Hero

The hero archetype is goal-driven and idealistic. The visualization exercise that works best for this masculine manifestation is journaling. Plot a journey of where you want to see yourself in one month, six months, one year, and then five years. Write down how you'll reach your goals and which obstacles you'll face along the way. Think about the external factors that can stop you and which flaws within yourself hold you back. Once you have your success mapped out, place it in a visible position where you can see it every day. Measure your progress and make the necessary adjustments to the plan whenever needed. Gamifying your life this way channels the masculine drive to push forward.

The Lover

The lover archetype is playful and pleasure-seeking. To alchemize your masculine essence through this highly feminine representation, you must find a way to transmute the mundane into magic. The sacred masculine is about productivity. Since you are drawn to passion, you must find a way to insert that passion into your goals. A simple way of doing this is by naming your tasks and referring to them as if they are people. For example, if you are a mechanic who works on cars, you can give your projects names like Jessica or Stephanie. When you speak or think about your projects, reframe the tasks as personified in your mind, like "I'm going to spend some time with Jessica today. She's been giving me issues, but we'll work through it." This way, you can channel the lover archetype into your goals and projects.

The Jester

The jester archetype is a joyful spirit that finds humor in life. Jesters can be tricky and manipulative pranksters that can often stir up inappropriate trouble. One of the best ways to masculinely channel the jester energy is by using a laughing meditation to start your day and tap into the playful essence of the cosmic giggle. Start by standing with your feet hips-width, stretching your hand up, and bending down to touch your toes. Next, shake your body and relax your facial muscles. You can give your jaw a light massage to relieve any pent-up tension. Stand facing forward in a comfortable position and then gently smile. Begin with a light giggle for a couple of minutes. Progressively laugh louder until you reach the peak of the crescendo with an outright thunderous guffaw. Finish the practice by lying down and being aware of all the feelings in your body and thoughts in your mind. Write down your thoughts for guidance on what to take action on and to gain clarity about your life's journey.

The Everyman

The everyman's superpower is the ability to relate to many different kinds of people and thus advocate for them. Due to the everyman being susceptible to falling into the trap of being overly swayed by the whims of other people, their meditations must ground them in their own identity. Doing a body scan is a brilliant meditation for the everyman to become more aligned with themselves outside of their social identity, making them better able to serve the community. Start by lying down flat on your back. Take a few deep breaths, and imagine a bright light that begins at the end of your toes. As you continue taking deep breaths, imagine the light slowly moving upwards from your toes to your feet and up towards your calves. Take note of how each part of your body feels as the light reaches it. Feel all the sensations as the light passes over it. Imagine it slowly moving upward over every part of your body while paying attention to how you feel. Once it reaches your head, it will disappear, and you will feel more in touch with your being.

The Caregiver

The caregiver is the nurturing archetype that puts themselves second for the sake of their loved ones or everyone around them. As the caregiver, much of your life is dedicated to society and the community. Your deeply empathetic drive informs all your decisions. A grounding meditation helps the caregiver root themselves into the material realm so that their subconscious can awaken to how they will serve the world. Sit with your back straight and your legs crossed or stretched out in front of you, depending on what is comfortable. Take a few deep breaths, then imagine a root growing from the bottom of your body deep into the earth. When the root reaches the center of the earth, it will wrap itself around a large multicolored crystal. The root will absorb the grounding energy from the crystal and bring it up to your body. This energy will slowly fill you up from your feet to the top of your head before exploding outward into the world.

The King

As a leader, the king must always be aware of the needs of those that they are ruling for their decisions to benefit those who rely on them. It is easy for this archetype to become blinded by their rigid view of the world, so staying in touch with the community is important. Therefore, integrity and understanding are essential traits for the king archetype to embody. Affirmations can keep a leader on a beneficial path. When you are getting ready in the morning, take a few deep breaths and repeat these mantras to yourself five times.

- I am focused.
- I have a responsibility to those I lead.
- I am compassionate, grounded, logical, and intelligent.
- My decisions are the best for the people under my leadership.
- I am open to advice and am wise enough to know what to reject and what to embrace for the benefit of the people I lead.
- I am dedicated, unselfish, and perfectly capable of tackling all hurdles that come my way.

The Creator

The creator archetype's function is to bring the new into existence. Therefore, if you are a creator, your meditations and visualizations should increase your creativity and channel that energy toward positive action in a sacred masculine existence. This archetype functions best when they tap into the flow state, a condition where you are absorbed by the activity you are doing as the world melts away. To regularly enter the flow state, you must curate your environment to optimize your creativity. Institute a ritual for your creative process. For example, organize your tools, take a few deep breaths, stretch your body, and have a cup of tea. Then, jump into your work and don't allow yourself to get distracted. This ritual you create should be personalized to you, so think about what makes you comfortable and productive.

The Innocent

The innocent is a trusting idealist committed to bringing about their perceived utopia. The innocent can be misled or taken advantage of due to their naive nature, but their intentions are always pure. The innocent is dedicated to creating a better, more peaceful world. To gain external peace, the innocent must maximize their peace. Therefore, a negativity-clearing meditation is beneficial for the innocent archetype. Sit down with your legs crossed and back straight. You can also extend your legs forward if that makes you feel more comfortable. Take a few deep breaths to start your practice. While breathing, imagine a bright white orb ascending down from heaven. This orb is made of positivity. It comes down and settles just above the top of your head. As you breathe in, particles of pure positivity break off from the orb, filling up your entire body. Visualize these particles, gathering all the black and sludgy negativity in your body. When you breathe out, the orb particles carry out the negativity and disperse it into the universe. Practice this meditation daily for at least 15 minutes.

The Sage

Sages are personifications of wisdom. They study, guide others, and master themselves through dedicated practice. The sage is the wise old man who has been through it all and sees through the folly of the world using a compassionate lens. A meditative practice that aligns with the sage is memorization. In Islam's religious tradition, individuals known as hafiz memorize the Holy Quran so that if the texts are ever destroyed, the tradition lives on through their breath. Decide on a text that resonates with you. It does not have to be long or religious. Practice memorizing it or a section of it daily and recite it each morning as part of a meditation.

The Explorer

The explorer is driven by thrills, always wanting to discover new things. This bravery serves society because the explorer can bring back knowledge and practice from their journeys or adventures to serve those around them. This adventurous energy can sometimes get reckless, so you need your sacred masculine to direct it productively. It helps to journal about your daily adventures and discoveries so you can draw the lessons out of the thrills you seek instead of mindlessly spinning from adrenaline rushes. Every night before bed, write about what you did that day and what you learned. This can add order and meaning to the chaos of adventure, transforming your restless seeking into character-building productivity.

Tools to Integrate Your Shadow

The shadow is a complex concept that can be easily misunderstood. It is misinterpreted as the negative side of an archetype. However, this is only partly true. Shadows represent darkness and keep things hidden. They should not merely be seen as unfavorable; instead, they should be thought of as *all the traits, thoughts, and motivations* people suppress and hide from the world. When you think of a shadow as *negative*, you make the mistake of inviting its destruction. The shadow is a part of yourself that will always be there, so it can never be truly destroyed. You need to integrate your shadow to become fully actualized in your sacred masculine. That means bringing the hidden aspects of yourself into the light in a way that can benefit you and those around you. Shadow work is not about killing the beast but taming it so it can help you harvest in the fields.

The Outlaw

The outlaw archetype is also known as the rebel because they fight against established systems they believe are incorrect, corrupt, or unjust. The outlaw shadow can manifest as nihilism and arrogance. To integrate the shadow of this archetype, your value system must be deeply explored, and you need to be open to working with people who are reforming a system from within the boundaries of the rules and regulations of the institution.

The Magician

The magician plays with reality to manifest dreams in the waking world. In ancient times, the Shaman embodied the magician, who walked the tightrope between this world and the next. The magician's understanding of the abstract makes their shadow manifest as manipulation. To integrate this shadow, the magician must use their powers of manipulation to reveal more profound truths to people around them instead of controlling them.

The Hero

Since the hero archetype is goal-orientated, they can often have extreme focus and tunnel vision. Therefore, the archetype's shadow manifests as a dedication to the wrong cause. Their loyalty can cause them to take negative actions, believing that they are in the right, like members of a white nationalist or terrorist organization. Therefore, the shadow of the hero is integrated by regularly reassessing your perceptions, values, and motivations.

The Lover

The lover archetype finds meaning in relationships, passion, and the pleasures of life. The lover's shadow is manipulation and deception because of their need to constantly fuel their pursuit of pleasure. To integrate the lover shadow, you need to transfer your passions into your projects as opposed to relationships to minimize the harm caused by your unsteady nature.

The Jester

The jester highlights the foolishness of reality by playfully pointing out the silliness of what most people take too seriously through jokes, pranks, and tricks. The jester shadow is deception. They need to find a way to channel this manipulative deception in a way that benefits themselves and others so that they don't become alienated. For example, the jester can use their playful and deceptive nature to teach.

The Everyman

The everyman is a chameleon that molds and blends themselves to fit into society. The shadow of the everyman is the fear of not fitting in or getting rejected. To integrate this shadow, the everyman must search within what matters most for them. From that vantage point, you can find a group that matches your desires and values and fits into the models that they represent.

The Caregiver

Caregivers in the shadow become victims or martyrs to the service of others. The way the caretaker's shadow gets integrated is by setting firm boundaries. Caretakers are naturally inclined to self-sacrifice for the service of others. However, people can often take advantage of this kind nature. The caretaker needs to be strict with whom they share their loving nature.

The King

The shadow of the king or ruler archetype is an overinflated ego expressed in authoritarian proclivities. Nobody wants people to know they have a higher opinion of themselves than those around them. The unbalanced ruler may suppress their narcissism and egoic expressions from others and themselves, hiding behind rigid rules that they feel they follow the best. The integration of the egoic shadow of the king is to strive to be the best person you can be and then bring others around you up to your level. Instead of assuming they can never be like you, ground yourself in the reality that everyone has valuable gifts you can unlock through effective leadership.

The Creator

The drive to create can cause instability when jumping from one project to the next. The creator's shadow can manifest in harsh self-judgment and not being able to see how brilliant their work is. To integrate the shadow of the creator, you need to organize your time and make sure that you finish your projects. You'll always judge your work harshly. By overcoming that fear, you will find that their feedback is most likely not as terrible as your own.

The Innocent

The innocent's idealism and positive outlook can hugely benefit a world filled with darkness. However, the inability to live in reality and take responsibility manifests in the shadow of dependency. Thus, the unbalanced innocent can attach themselves to the idealistic views of a manipulatively abusive person. Integrating the shadow of the innocent requires the acceptance of failure as an opportunity to learn. Getting attached to different people or groups will result in your fingers getting burnt, but you must resiliently build yourself up from this as a dominantly innocent archetype.

The Sage

The sage is wise and often represented in mythology as an old man. Due to their understanding of the world, the sage's shadow can manifest as emotionally detached, rigid, and overly critical. To integrate this shadow, the sage must take on students whom they can learn from in their teaching relationships. Correcting a student is welcomed, but being hyper-critical of random individuals can be isolating.

The Explorer

The explorer's shadow manifests through their desire to always find something new. This creates escapist qualities that can become apparent through substance abuse or unfiltered thrill-seeking, which prevents them from establishing strong bonds. To integrate the shadow of the explorer, you need to turn the mundane into an adventure. This means finding new ways to do old things so that your mind is always engaged with the novelty of everyday life, which prevents escapism.

Harmonizing the Intersections of Your Archetypes

It is unlikely that the entirety of your being will just slip neatly into one archetypal figure. People are layered beings that function in multiple complex ways. Your archetypal expressions may be contradictory and paradoxical. The only way you can harmonize the intersections of the various archetypes you embody is by doing the inner work to identify which archetypes show up in which scenarios or contexts in your life. For example, you may embody the caregiver at home with your family and at work act as the ruler while being more of the jester in social environments. Understanding the layers of yourself requires mindful practices so you can sort through the mess of your internal environment and order it with the sacred masculine.

Mindfulness to Awaken the Masculine

In light of understanding the integrations of your shadow and the harmonizing of your intersecting archetypes, mindfulness is one of the most valuable practices that you can use to awaken the sacred masculine. Mindfulness means being present fully at the moment without judgment or attachment. This helps the sacred masculine because it can focus on one task at a time and push through until it is completed. Many practices enhance your mindfulness, but the best way to integrate it through the divine masculine into your life every day is by living in the moment and focusing on one task at a time. Meditation does not have to be sitting with closed eyes, crossed legs, and breathing while chanting a mantra. These mindful exercises are beneficial, but you can expand your practice by using your everyday tasks as meditations. For example, do not allow your mind to drift off when you are cleaning. When you catch your mind wandering, bring it back to focus on the task at hand. Being mindful then becomes a lifestyle instead of a practice, which gives the divine masculine space to develop and grow through disciplined control of the mind and asserted action.

Chapter 4: Inner Strength and Courage

Inner strength and courage are two of the most fundamental aspects of sacred masculine energy. They are two hearts pumping life into the divine masculine. Without them, the concept would devolve into nothingness and eventually transform into all the negative aspects of masculinity, like dominance and aggression. After all, the weak tend to be aggressive, and the cowardly need to assert their dominance. Before you get down to harnessing these two vital qualities, it's essential to understand their core meaning.

Inner strength and courage are two of the most fundamental aspects of sacred masculine energy.[46]

Inner Strength

Inner strength is your power that cannot be seen but felt. If used well, it can turn out to be one of the brightest areas of your divine masculine. It is mental and emotional, a unique energy flowing through your entire being. It affects three major parts of your sacred masculine energy:

1. Emotional Resilience

It can build your emotional resilience so you can respond to any situation instead of simply reacting to it. For example, if a long-standing, trusted client at work suddenly calls you and ends the contract, your initial reaction will be shock. Confusion follows, and when you are ready to face the client and understand their motivations so you can try to get them back, they are long gone. Emotional resilience allows you to recover from shock and confusion to proceed to salvage the situation.

2. Mental Fortitude

Inner strength develops another critical skill: mental fortitude. It is a measure of your mental toughness and resilience when your physical strength gives way. It is especially useful in sports and other physical activities. When you are playing soccer and have a clear shot at the goal but are completely exhausted and simply cannot take another step, your mental fortitude gives you the required energy to kick the ball. When you push yourself while working out, how do you manage to get in just another rep or run that extra mile each day? It's all thanks to your mental fortitude.

3. Perseverance

Perseverance, especially in the face of adversity, is a difficult skill to acquire. How do you keep going when everything is acting against you? How do you stand firm against an incoming avalanche of problems? Your inner strength kicks into action at such times, giving you the power to persevere so you can face any challenge head-on. It gives you enough strength to keep at it despite all the odds. The result may not always be in your favor, but self-satisfaction is assured.

Courage

Courage is not about being overly brave or immune to fear. It is about plodding on despite your fears. Fear is a perfectly natural emotional state, but courage is an acquired quality. The ability to face your fears and move forward is extremely powerful in people with a strong sense of the divine masculine. Courage can manifest in three different forms:

1. Moral Courage

This pertains primarily to your moral inclinations and is different for different people. When you are faced with a moral or ethical dilemma, do you stand by your values regardless of the consequences? Do you possess the strength to go against popular opinion? Moral courage is the ability to take a morally right action against all odds. For instance, if someone else is being reprimanded for a mistake you made, are you able to speak the truth? How about addressing an injustice in society when nobody else is doing so?

Moral courage is not easy to come by. People often prefer to go against their morality instead of standing strong, which makes sense in certain situations. You need to carefully weigh the situation's pros and cons before deciding. Moral courage isn't about impulsively or reflexively showing bravery. That's called a defense mechanism. Moral courage is all about thinking clearly and assessing the situation before taking action.

2. Physical Courage

This is the kind of courage you often see in action movies. When the protagonist keeps doing what's right without caring about physical hardships or death threats, they show physical courage. It is an endangered quality rarely found in today's world. Ask yourself the following questions, and answer honestly:

- Would you protect someone against an armed assailant?
- Would you rescue someone from a burning building?
- Would you prevent a crime from being committed when no one else is around?
- Would you report a crime under threat from a criminal?

If you answered "yes" to all these questions, your physical courage is right up there with action movie protagonists, which makes your sacred masculine energy shine intensely bright.

3. Confronting Inner Fears

Being courageous is not about being fearless but confronting your fears. Everyone is afraid of something. Your fear may be obscure, like being afraid of an octopus. You don't come across many octopuses in day-to-day life, so you simply ignore that fear. However, it still lingers within you, and you never know what form it may take in the future. The sacred masculine energy gives you the courage to face that fear head-on.

It becomes especially important if your fear is something common, like being afraid of heights. Don't find yourself in a situation where you end up at the peak of a mountain to face your fear of heights. Tap into your divine masculine energy and deliberately put yourself in a situation where you can confront your fears. This way, at least, you'll be well prepared for it.

In courage lies the secret to unlocking your potential to make difficult decisions. A number of new choices open up before you, ones you may never have thought about before. You acquire the power to make a difficult choice, especially if it is the right one. After making that choice, courage lends you the potential to go through with your decision without being afraid of the consequences. In short, it helps you take bold actions you may not choose to do under normal circumstances, like facing your fear of heights by climbing down the mountain's peak instead of waiting for someone to save you.

The Deep Connection between Strength and Courage

Inner strength and courage, the two pillars of sacred masculine energy, are deeply connected physically, emotionally, and spiritually. You will find the courage to undertake difficult tasks if you possess inner strength. Similarly, you'll find the strength for the purpose if you dare to face your fears; there isn't one without the other.

Say you notice a thief trying to snatch a passerby's purse on an otherwise deserted street. The thief is armed with a knife and is better built than you. You have the physical courage to take them on but not the required strength. Your common sense will prompt you to call the cops, but by the time they arrive, the thief would have done the deed and run off, maybe even knifing the passerby.

At this moment, as you muster the courage to confront the thief, your hardened resolve will lend you the strength to do so. Your emotional resilience will grow and prompt you to take action. As your physical energy drains, your mental fortitude will come to your rescue, and you'll find the inner strength to persevere. And who knows, seeing your courage and resolve, the victim might also help.

Scenarios and Contexts

How will you know when to show courage and use your inner strength? The scenarios that demand these two divine masculine qualities are not easily recognizable. You may have already used them in the past to tackle some problem or failed to use them because you didn't know you possessed these powerhouses of sacred masculinity. Here are a few relatable scenarios and contexts where you can implement your newfound powers.

Major Scenarios

- **You Have Lost a Loved One and Are Finding It Difficult to Move on.** Overcoming a trauma will be one of the greatest tests of your inner strength. Their memories may keep haunting you, and you may even (falsely) blame yourself for their death. Your inner strength will give you the power to let go. It doesn't mean you'll forget them. You will cherish their fond memories and celebrate their life, but their passing away will never hold you back.

- **You Have Failed Far Too Many Times and Wish to End Everything.** This will be the greatest battle of your life, for your life: you against you. Clinical depression is a serious illness that can be overcome with the help of the divine masculine. Two of the most effective medicines for hopelessness are your inner strength and courage. Giving up on life means you have lost the courage to live, implying that your inner strength is at an all-time low. Develop the strength to try again and gather the courage to fail again. Success won't be too far off.

- **You Have Experienced a Shocking Incident.** You may think that recovering from an accident is entirely physical. It is a proven fact in physiotherapy that your mental state of mind is equally important for making a full recovery. You are filled with negative thoughts and emotions after experiencing something devastating. Your inner strength holds the power to transform them into positive feelings, encouraging you to dwell less on the past and focus more on the future. In turn, your courage helps you face that shocking incident and accept your circumstances to begin healing.

- **You Are About to Do the Most Important Thing in Your Life.** It can be anything, from sitting for an interview for your dream job or launching your startup to breaking up a long relationship or marrying the love of your life. During these turning points in life, your inner strength is tested. You may have been ready to marry for years, but when that day finally comes, you may not want to go through with it. This sudden change is called a number of things, like pre-wedding jitters or nerves, and it is completely normal. One of the reasons it happens is because of your faltering inner strength. You are probably thinking about the future too much. Focus on your present, and both those aspects of your being will return.

The Little Things

You don't have to wait for major events to explore your inner strength and courage. Practice with the little things that you encounter every day. Building your confidence and resilience takes time to gather courage and strength.

- Walk to work instead of taking your car or public transport. A bit of exercise every morning gives you the energy to go through the day.
- When faced with any minor ethical dilemma at work, don't take the easy way out. Do the right thing. For instance, if your subordinates already have a lot of work on their hands and your boss gives you some more, try to do it yourself or explain the situation to your boss. Both these choices require inner strength and courage. The easy (and wrong) way out would be to assign the extra work to your subordinates.
- If you find a homeless person having a heart attack on the street, don't think twice before administering CPR or calling an ambulance. Apart from being your duty as a human being, the act also tests your inner strength because people normally won't do anything to help the homeless or weak.
- After a hard day's work, go home with a smile on your face. Don't bring your work home. Your family and children may have had to endure their own set of problems. Listen to their complaints and woes. Show genuine interest in what they have to

say. It requires a different kind of courage to show genuine happiness when you are in pain.

Embodiment Exercises

Once awakened, your sacred masculine energy is relatively easier to maintain than the connection between your mind and body. Your mind strengthens your body and vice versa, but if your senses are not in touch with either one, you'll lose the connection and, in turn, the power of the divine masculine. Part of the reason why you cannot bring yourself to help your fellow humans or take morally sound actions is the lack of the mind-body connection.

Embodiment is the act of getting in touch with your mind and body and feeling the world through your physical, emotional, and spiritual senses. Your thoughts and your physical being are interconnected, and embodiment helps you explore that link. It can be something as simple as touching the space around you with the palms of your hands. Simple acts like these will help you forge a better relationship with your mind and body and, eventually, with your sacred masculine energy.

Easy Breathing

Breathing comes naturally to you, but when you focus on it, you get in touch with your inner consciousness, your mind. Practice breathing for a few minutes each day.

1. Breathe in. Feel yourself inhaling the positive energy around you. Imagine that it's boosting your inner strength and amplifying your courage.
2. Hold for a few seconds. Revel in your increased strength and courage.
3. Breathe out slowly. Feel the negative energy escape as you exhale. Let go of all your regrets, mistakes, and inhibitions.
4. Hold for a few seconds. Relish your freedom from the negativity.

Ultra-Focused Breathing

In this simple breathing exercise, you'll learn to feel where the air travels within your body.

1. Start with easy breathing. Get your mind to focus.
2. Take a deep breath. Feel the air travel through your nostrils, down your throat, and into your lungs. Feel your chest rise and your

ribcage expand.
3. Without pulling up your shoulders, pucker your lips and breathe out slowly. Feel your belly contract as your lungs go back to their original size.
4. When you think you can no longer exhale, use your belly muscles to blow out whatever air remains.

You'll have to deliberately repeat this twice or thrice, after which you'll naturally experience those feelings as you focus.

Grounding Techniques

These are similar to breathing exercises but are on a more physical level. Are incessant negative thoughts stopping you from connecting with the divine masculine? Grounding techniques will help you focus on the present moment instead of thinking about those negative thoughts.

- Use the 5-4-3-2-1 technique to get in touch with your surroundings. Acknowledge and describe five things you can see, four things you can touch, three things you can hear, two things you can smell, and one thing you can taste.
- Pick an object in your environment and focus on it. Pay attention to its color, shape, texture, and any other details. Close your eyes and try to sketch it in your mind's eye. This helps shift your focus away from distressing thoughts.
- Hold any object in your hand, like a stone, and close your eyes. Feel its texture down to the tiniest notch. Try to determine its shape. Is it oval or circular? Is it hard or smooth? Are there any jagged edges?
- Sit or stand comfortably and close your eyes. Imagine roots growing from the soles of your feet into the ground, grounding you. Feel the stability and support as you visualize these roots. Anxiety and negative thoughts often take over when you feel you have no support. This rooting exercise gives you that much-needed grounding support.
- Name or count the objects in your vicinity. Pick them up as you go for a better grounding presence. This helps you focus your mind on the present moment and takes your attention away from anxious thoughts.

- Close your eyes and take a few deep breaths. Imagine inhaling a calming color, like blue, and exhaling a stressful color, like red. Picture the calming color filling your body and pushing out the stressful color. This color breathing exercise is similar to easy breathing but more imaginative.
- Close your eyes and visualize a peaceful place. Engage all your senses in this visualization, imagining the sights, sounds, smells, and textures. How do the trees look, the flowers smell, and the fruits taste? What does the surface you're standing on feel like? How high-pitched are the birds' sounds?

Emotional and Spiritual Body Check

This is a slightly more advanced technique. It involves focusing on each part of your body, identifying the stressful areas, and de-stressing them. Start by focusing on your head. Take a deep breath and see if you notice any tension in your head or face. Do your eyes feel jittery? Are your lips pursed too tightly? Is there a bit of pain in your forehead? As you identify each stressor, try to release that tension and untie those knots with steady breathing. Repeat the same exercise with your throat, chest, diaphragm, belly, and pelvis.

Yoga

Embodied yoga is an approach that emphasizes the integration of mind and body, bringing awareness to the present moment through movement, breath, and mindful awareness. It goes beyond the physical postures (asanas) commonly associated with yoga and focuses on cultivating a deep connection with your body, sensations, and emotions. You have to focus not only on your breath but also on every part of your body. It ensures that you develop physical as well as inner strength. Two easy asanas (poses/exercises) you can try are:
- **Virabhadrasana (Warrior Pose):** It's similar to the lunges exercise, with one leg bent in the front and the other leg stretched behind. Keep your upper body perpendicular to the ground and your arms stretched upward. Hold this pose for as long as you can.

Warrior pose.[47]

- Tadasana (Mountain Pose): This is almost the same as stretching your body while standing. With the fingers of both your hands interlocked above your head, stretch yourself as far as you can without bending backward. Stand on your toes to facilitate a better stretch.

You can ideally do this with any other type of exercise, like tai chi or kung fu.

Mountain pose.[48]

Chapter 5: Clarity of Mind and Focus

During your spiritual and personal development journey, following the divine masculine archetype can instill qualities that embody strength, decisiveness, and purpose. Likewise, having a conscious mind and excellent focus is necessary to develop these divine masculine abilities, become self-aware, and live a good life.

Having a conscious mind can be understood as your heightened state of awareness where your conscious and subconscious mind remains unclouded by confusion or distraction. This state of mental lucidity allows you to navigate thoughts and emotions with precision, unveiling a deeper understanding of life's purpose and values. When embodying the divine masculine archetype, your clarity of mind becomes the torchbearer, illuminating the path toward meaningful existence.

A conscious mind and excellent focus are necessary to develop these divine masculine abilities.[49]

Similarly, focus on a divine masculine context is the ability to concentrate on tasks and a strong commitment to undivided attention toward purposeful goals and milestones. It's the focus that will allow you to channel your mental energy into specific goals, cut through the clutter, and be determined to pursue your aspirations and objectives with unwavering intent.

In this chapter, you'll read about direct attention, purposeful action, concentration on meaningful objectives, decisiveness in decision-making, and harmonization with higher values to improve your clarity and focus. You'll also learn the neurological intricacies and psychological dynamics that underpin these virtues, providing a comprehensive understanding of how they can shape your journey toward spiritual and personal fulfillment.

Directed Attention

It's the intentional focus on mental energy towards a certain task or goal. It's a cognitive process (learning process) where you consciously choose to concentrate on a particular activity, filtering out irrelevant stimuli and inhibiting distractions. This cognitive process relies on the brain's executive functions, particularly the prefrontal cortex, which is involved in decision-making and sustained attention. Neurotransmitters like dopamine aid in regulating attention, and the brain's neural networks adapt to reinforce the chosen focus. This deliberate act of attentional control enables you to engage more with the present moment, enhancing cognitive performance and promoting a sense of mindfulness.

Purposeful Action

It's a deliberate behavior fueled by a clear understanding of your core values and overarching goals. This involves consciously aligning actions with a higher purpose or meaningful objective. Neurologically, purposeful action is linked to the region in the brain responsible for goal-setting and the reward system. The brain's ventral striatum responds to the anticipation of rewards associated with purposeful actions, making the connection stronger between your behavior and intrinsic motivations. Likewise, the prefrontal cortex, responsible for decision-making, planning, and self-control, shapes purposeful actions by integrating long-term goals with immediate choices.

Concentration on Meaningful Goals

An understanding of personal values and unwavering commitment is necessary to concentrate on meaningful objectives and goals. When you are determined to perform a task or strive to achieve a goal, the goal-related neural circuits activate in the dorsal lateral prefrontal cortex, an area associated with cognitive control and working memory. Besides the activation of these neural circuits, the brain's reward system activates, releasing neurotransmitters like serotonin and endorphins to reinforce the sense of accomplishment associated with progress toward meaningful goals. Furthermore, cognitive flexibility, facilitated by the anterior cingulate cortex, allows you to adapt your strategies when faced with challenges, maintaining focus on the overarching objectives.

Decisiveness in Decision-Making

Decisiveness is all about making prompt and confident decisions, unencumbered by indecision or doubt. At a neural level, decision-making involves various brain regions like the orbitofrontal cortex, which evaluates options based on reward and punishment, and the amygdala, responsible for processing emotions related to choices. The intricate balance between these regions, connected through neural pathways, leads to decisive decision-making. The hippocampus also becomes active, integrating past experiences into refining decision-making and ensuring adaptability.

Harmonizing with Higher Values

Harmonizing with higher values changes your ego for good, aligning actions with universal principles like the ones instilled in the divine masculine archetype. In medical terms, cognitive processes like these engage areas of the brain associated with social cognition, empathy, and moral reasoning. Likewise, the mirror neuron system makes you resonate with the experiences and emotions of others, promoting interconnectedness. The prefrontal cortex is also actively involved in moral decision-making, guiding you to make choices that contribute to the greater good. The brain's reward system further promotes intrinsic satisfaction when your actions match with higher values, creating a sense of fulfillment and purpose.

Each aspect of focus and clarity of mind within the framework of the divine masculine involves intricate neurological processes, engaging various brain regions, neurotransmitters, and cognitive functions. Understanding these mechanisms reveals a comprehensive view of how the mind navigates directed attention, purposeful action, concentration on goals that matter, and decisiveness in decision-making, all in harmony with higher values.

Common Mental Obstacles and Strategies for Overcoming Challenges

Procrastination

This is one of the most problematic obstacles that keeps you from growing, transforming, and giving things your all. Procrastination results from a mix of psychological factors, which mostly include the fear of failure, perfectionism, or a lack of motivation. The brain's limbic system, responsible for regulating emotions, deals with procrastination by triggering avoidance behaviors and minimizing the negative effects associated with challenging tasks.

Strategies for Dealing with Procrastination

- **Temporal Motivation Theory**: This theory states that the motivation you harness to do a certain task is influenced by the perceived value of the task and your expectancy of success. In simple words, the more confidence you have in succeeding, the more motivated you'll be to do the task.

- **Implementation Intention**: This strategy is based on forming a solid plan by specifying when, where, and how a task will be accomplished. You'll be using your prefrontal cortex to brainstorm and create a mental script to streamline the initiation of a task.

- **Cognitive Restructuring**: Rewiring your brain by addressing irrationality helps reshape negative thought patterns, contributing positively to procrastination. In cognitive restructuring, you'll face self-defeating thoughts and replace them with realistic and positive ones.

Self-Doubt

It's a cognitive phenomenon where you doubt your abilities and see them in a negative light. Past failures, perceived inadequacies, and fear of judgment mostly trigger self-doubt. The amygdala triggers self-doubt responses, sometimes taking you on an emotional rollercoaster.

Strategies for Dealing with Self-Doubt

- **Positive Affirmations**: According to psychology, listening, reading, and repeating positive affirmations stimulate the reward center in the brain, releasing dopamine and reinforcing positive self-perceptions. Neural pathways in the brain can be reshaped over time to counteract self-doubt through tailored positive affirmations. When searching for positive affirmations, pick the ones that align with the most important things and the core values.

- **Visualization Techniques**: This technique involves training your motor and visual cortex, training the brain by creating a mental rehearsal of success. Vividly imagining positive outcomes fosters a sense of self-efficacy, activating areas associated with confidence and motivation.
- **Self-Compassion Practices**: This practice includes drawing from principles of self-compassion, treating yourself with the same kindness and understanding you would offer to a friend. Being self-compassionate triggers soothing effects, reducing the impact of self-critical thoughts.

Distractions

There are two types of distractions: external, which includes any stimuli in the environment, and internal, which mostly consists of your thoughts. The brain's prefrontal cortex is the region responsible for regulating attention and maintaining focus.

Strategies for Dealing with Distractions

- **Reorganizing environments**: Optimizing your surroundings at home and your workspace can reduce visual and auditory stimuli that may divert your attention. Environments with low auditory and visual stimuli calm the brain's processing areas and aid in sustaining focus.
- **Task-Switching Costs**: The brain incurs a cost when switching between tasks. Recognize the toll you will be paying when switching tasks and encourage yourself to focus on a single task for more extended periods, promoting efficiency and minimizing mental fatigue.

Lack of Clear Goals

Without clear goals, you won't be motivated as much, and your actions may show a lack of direction. The brain's frontal lobes, responsible for executive functions like goal-setting, can struggle to initiate actions when objectives are ambiguous.

Strategies for Dealing with a Lack of Clear Goals

- **Executive Function Activation:** The prefrontal cortex can activate executive functions when clear goals are set. Clearly defining goals and breaking them down into achievable and actionable steps keeps the prefrontal cortex stimulated, facilitating clearer decision-making and sustained motivation. As you've read earlier in this chapter, your brain's reward center will also respond to these clear goals, releasing dopamine and reinforcing motivation.
- **Goal Visualization:** Similar to self-doubt strategies, visualizing yourself achieving goals creates a positive feedback loop that reinforces goal-directed behaviors. Your understanding of these mental obstacles and implementing strategies to cope with these issues will eventually lead to a more focused and resilient mindset.

Mental Clarity and Health

It's a no-brainer that physical well-being and mental clarity are interconnected. If there's an issue with your health, your mental focus, attention, and thought patterns won't be the same. Fortunately, various lifestyle practices like adequate exercise, balanced nutrition, enough sleep, and several others can be incorporated into daily life to promote mental and physical well-being.

Exercise and Mental Clarity

When you exercise regularly, mental clarity and cognitive function improve. Besides pumping the muscles and increasing blood flow to the heart to make it stronger, exercise triggers the release of neurotransmitters, including dopamine and serotonin. These neurotransmitters regulate mood and enhance attention. While brisk walking, jogging, or a workout will work, incorporating aerobic exercises in your routine promotes blood flow to the brain, delivering the essential nutrients for optimal cognitive performance.

Nutrition and Cognitive Function

Proper nutrition is fundamental for sustaining energy levels and supporting cognitive function. The brain requires a balanced supply of nutrients, including omega-3 fatty acids, antioxidants, vitamins, and minerals. Foods rich in these nutrients, like fatty fish, fruits, vegetables, and whole grains, must be included for optimal brain health. Just like you'll add these nutritious foods to your diet, avoid excessive consumption of processed foods, sugar, and caffeine to prevent energy crashes and support sustained mental focus.

Adequate Rest and Cognitive Performance

Quality sleep is indispensable for mental clarity and cognitive function. During sleep, the brain undergoes various processes like memory consolidation, neural repair, and toxin removal. Lack of sufficient sleep will only impair attention, decision-making, and problem-solving abilities. Try establishing a consistent sleep schedule, creating a conducive sleep environment, and practicing relaxation techniques for a restful and rejuvenating sleep.

Hydration and Cognitive Function

Dehydration has noticeable effects on cognitive function. Even mild dehydration makes it difficult to concentrate and increases fatigue. Staying adequately hydrated provides the brain with a constant supply of necessary fluids to maintain optimal function.

Stress Management and Mental Clarity

Chronic stress can detrimentally impact mental clarity, leading to cognitive fatigue and impaired decision-making. Practices like mindfulness meditation, deep breathing exercises, and progressive muscle relaxation effectively reduce stress levels and can be incorporated into your exercise routine for better stress management. These soothing techniques activate the parasympathetic nervous system, promoting a sense of calm and clarity in the mind. You'll read about these practices in detail in the mindful practices section.

Regular Breaks and Cognitive Renewal

Lastly, regular breaks during work or study sessions are essential for preventing mental fatigue and sustaining focus. The brain operates optimally in cycles of focused activity followed by short breaks. You can include activities like stretching, walking, and even taking naps when necessary to rejuvenate the mind, priming it to perform the next task with enhanced mental clarity.

The body and mind are intricately connected. Maintaining mental clarity is foundational to taking care of and enhancing your physical well-being. A holistic approach works best as it combines regular exercise, balanced nutrition, sufficient rest, stress management, hydration, and mindful breaks.

Mindfulness Practices

Stress Reduction

Mindfulness practices are well-known for their stress-reducing benefits. Deep breathing and various forms of meditation can activate the body's relaxation response, leading to a decrease in stress hormones. This reduced stress facilitates mental clarity by alleviating the mental fog associated with heightened stress levels.

Besides stress reduction, you'll develop stress resilience when you have a heightened awareness of thoughts and emotions. This resilience enables a calm and composed mindset, preventing stress from derailing your mental clarity and navigating challenges.

Emotional Regulation

One of the foundational pillars of mindfulness practices is to analyze your observations and thoughts without judgment. This practice takes you to a higher state of mental awareness, allowing you to regulate emotions more effectively. The emotional stability you'll harness from this practice gives you mental clarity and prevents overwhelming emotions from clouding judgment and decision-making.

Enhanced Creativity

Moments of stillness provide a fertile ground for creativity to flourish. You can access novel ideas and solutions by quieting the mind and allowing it to wander without external distractions. This creative enhancement contributes to a more expansive and innovative perspective, ultimately benefiting mental clarity.

Increased Self-Awareness

Mindfulness practices promote self-awareness by encouraging you to observe your thoughts, feelings, and behaviors without attachment. Staying in the present moment reduces the tendency to become distracted by irrelevant thoughts or external stimuli. As a result, channeling attention becomes easier and more effective. This heightened self-awareness allows for a clearer understanding of personal values, goals, and motivations, guiding actions and decisions with greater purpose and intention.

Enhanced Decision-Making

Clear moments of stillness provide a mental space where you can approach decision-making with a calm and focused mind. By reducing mental clutter and external noise, you can make decisions more thoughtfully and with greater clarity, resulting in more informed and strategic choices.

Improved Sleep Quality

Meditation and mindfulness practices that involve relaxation techniques can exponentially improve sleep quality. Adequate and quality sleep is vital for a clear mind and cognitive functions. You can create a short meditation routine before bedtime to improve your sleep experience.

These practical and effective practices offer a holistic sense of well-being. Incorporate mindfulness practices to enhance focus, improve mental clarity, and reduce stress to experience an improved quality of life. This sense of well-being permeates various aspects of daily living, promoting a positive outlook and a resilient mindset.

Getting Inspired

Drawing inspiration from masculine archetypes adds a rich and symbolic dimension when you are striving to achieve a heightened state of focus and a clear understanding of your path and life purpose. Here are some examples of archetypal figures to draw inspiration from and set your path toward achieving ultimate focus and clarity of mind.

The Sage's Wisdom and Insight

Understanding Inner Wisdom

The Sage archetype, deeply rooted in various cultural and mythological traditions, represents the embodiment of wisdom and insight. To draw inspiration from the Sage for mental clarity, you can delve into practices that cultivate inner wisdom. Meditation, a cornerstone of many ancient traditions, allows for a profound exploration of the mind's depths. Regular meditation gives you access to their inner well of knowledge and intuition, contributing to heightened mental clarity.

Seeking Purpose-Driven Knowledge

The Sage's pursuit of knowledge is purpose-driven. Instead of merely accumulating facts, you can adopt a mindset akin to the Sage by seeking knowledge that aligns with your life purpose. This purpose-driven quest ensures that every piece of acquired wisdom has relevance and contributes to a clear understanding of one's path.

Reflective Practices for Clarity

The Sage often engages in reflective practices to distill wisdom from life experiences. Emulating this archetype involves incorporating journaling, philosophical contemplation, or discussions with wise mentors into daily life. These practices encourage introspection and self-awareness, facilitating a clear understanding of personal values and the path forward.

The Warrior's Concentrated and Determined Mindset

Focused Attention on Goals

The Warrior archetype exemplifies concentrated determination. In the context of mental clarity, you can adopt a Warrior's mindset by setting clear and compelling goals. This focused attention on specific objectives eliminates distractions and creates a mental environment conducive to concentration and purposeful action.

Discipline and Routine

Warriors are renowned for their discipline and commitment to rigorous training. Translating this into daily life involves establishing disciplined routines. Whether it's a structured work schedule, a consistent physical exercise regimen, or dedicated mindfulness practices, routines instill discipline and build the mental resilience necessary for sustained concentration.

Overcoming Obstacles with Resilience

The Warrior faces challenges with resilience and courage. Applying this mindset means viewing obstacles as opportunities for growth rather than insurmountable barriers. This perspective shifts the focus from problems to solutions, contributing to mental clarity by cultivating a proactive and determined approach to life's challenges.

The Explorer's Curiosity and Adaptability

Curiosity as a Driving Force

The Explorer archetype embodies an insatiable curiosity and a thirst for adventure. To harness this quality for mental clarity, you can approach life with a curious mindset. Actively seeking new ideas, experiences, and perspectives stimulates the mind, preventing stagnation and contributing to a continuous learning process that fosters mental clarity.

Adaptability in the Face of Change

Explorers thrive in diverse environments and easily adapt to change. Applying this quality involves developing adaptability in response to life's changes. An adaptable mindset supports mental clarity by minimizing resistance to change. Instead of being overwhelmed by uncertainty, with an Explorer's adaptability, you can navigate the twists and turns of their path with resilience and an open mind.

Integrating elements from the Sage, Warrior, and Explorer archetypes involves a profound journey of self-discovery and intentional practice. Through meditation, purpose-driven knowledge-seeking, disciplined routines, resilience in the face of challenges, and a curiosity-driven approach to life, you can cultivate a mindset that aligns with these archetypal qualities, contributing to extreme mental clarity and a purposeful life journey. Although it will take time to understand the intricacies and develop an inner personality that portrays the earlier mentioned qualities and to achieve the purpose in life you aim for.

Chapter 6: Becoming a Leader

Effective leadership is a dynamic concoction of qualities and traits beyond mere managerial skills. A successful leader perfectly balances traits like strength, vision, and decision-making with integrity, humility, and empathy. They develop and strive to incorporate attributes that contribute to their ability to inspire and guide others. In this chapter, you'll read about key qualities associated with successful leaders, exploring the nuances and interconnections that leave an impact. Understanding the intricacies of leadership traits makes it easier to comprehend that leaders with divine masculine energy won't have a problem creating purpose-driven and compassionate environments conducive to growth and achievement.

Effective leadership is a dynamic concoction of qualities and traits beyond mere managerial skills.⁵⁰

Traits of Successful Leaders

Physical Strength

In leadership roles, physical strength may not necessarily refer to literal physical prowess but rather to the resilience and endurance leaders exhibit in the face of challenges. It involves persevering through difficulties, maintaining stamina during demanding periods, and serving as a steadfast example.

Emotional Strength

Leadership often involves navigating complex and emotionally charged situations. Emotional strength is the ability to remain composed under pressure, handle criticism gracefully, and manage personal emotions effectively. Leaders with emotional strength are better equipped to make rational decisions, provide stability during turbulent times, and create a positive emotional climate around them.

Strategic Thinking

Successful leaders are distinguished by their strategic thinking abilities. That involves having a clear vision of the future and the capacity to devise comprehensive strategies to achieve long-term goals. Strategic thinking enables leaders to anticipate challenges, identify opportunities, and delegate purposefully toward a shared vision. It's a forward-looking mindset that aligns actions with overarching objectives, enabling organizational growth and sustainability.

Innovation

Visionary leaders are not only focused on existing goals but are also open to innovation. They encourage creativity within their teams, embracing new ideas and approaches to problem-solving. By practicing a culture of innovation, leaders ensure that their organizations remain dynamic and responsive to evolving challenges.

Decisiveness

Decisiveness is a fundamental aspect of effective leadership. Successful leaders make timely and well-informed decisions, even in the face of uncertainty. A decisive leader instills confidence in the team, maintains momentum, and ensures that opportunities are not missed. This quality is crucial for navigating complex situations, enabling leaders to take bold actions with clarity and purpose.

Accountability

Decision-making is accompanied by accountability in successful leadership. Leaders take responsibility for the outcomes of their decisions, whether positive or negative. This accountability promotes trust with everyone around. It also sets the stage for continuous improvement as leaders learn from successful outcomes and setbacks.

Honesty

Integrity is the bedrock of successful leadership, and honesty is a cornerstone of this quality. Leaders build trust by communicating transparently and authentically. Honest leaders are respected for their sincerity, and their actions align with their words. That creates a foundation of trust within the team and establishes the leader as a reliable and conscientious figure.

Consistency

Maintaining consistency in values and actions is integral to leadership integrity. Consistent leaders earn credibility by aligning their decisions and behaviors with a set of ethical principles. This consistency creates a sense of predictability and reliability, reinforcing followers' trust in their leader.

Openness to Feedback

Humble leaders actively seek and welcome feedback. They understand they don't have all the answers and are open to learning from others. This openness creates a culture of continuous improvement, where constructive criticism is seen as an opportunity for growth rather than a threat. By valuing the input of others, humble leaders foster a collaborative and inclusive work environment.

Understanding

Empathetic leaders demonstrate a deep understanding of their peers' needs, concerns, and perspectives. This understanding goes beyond surface-level interactions and involves actively listening to individuals, acknowledging their experiences, and considering their feelings. Leaders who cultivate empathy create a supportive work environment where everyone feels valued and understood.

Compassion

Beyond understanding, empathetic leaders express compassion for the well-being of their team members. Compassionate leaders create a sense of belonging and trust, as team members know their leader genuinely cares about their success and happiness.

Clarity

Leaders articulate their vision, expectations, and objectives in a manner easily understood by their team. Clear communication minimizes misunderstandings, aligns everyone towards common goals, and facilitates a cohesive and focused work environment.

Active Listening

Leaders who actively listen create an inclusive and collaborative culture. This two-way communication approach enhances problem-solving, innovation, and the team's overall well-being.

Risk-Taking

Courageous leaders are willing to take calculated risks in pursuit of organizational goals. Risk-taking drives innovation, explores new opportunities, and challenges the status quo.

Resilience

Resilient leaders bounce back from adversity, demonstrating a steadfast commitment to their vision and goals. Resilience boosts confidence in unfavorable times and sets the tone for a positive and determined organizational culture.

Examining these qualities and traits in detail gives you a clear picture of the multifaceted nature of successful leadership. These attributes are not isolated. Instead, they interact and complement each other, shaping leaders who can navigate complexities, inspire people around them, and contribute to holistic growth.

Exploring Divine Masculine Leadership

Leadership roles inspired by the divine masculine energy require a solid integration of strength, vision, and compassion. Drawing inspiration from this energy, you can embody a leadership style that transcends conventional paradigms. The divine masculine principles guide leaders toward a balanced expression of power, purpose, and empathy. It involves recognizing the inherent strength in vulnerability, the vision in compassion, and the power in humility. Leaders attuned to the divine masculine principles become facilitators of growth, creating and supporting environments where both individual and collective potential blooms.

Transformational Leadership

Transformational leadership aligns closely with the principles of the divine masculine. This leadership style follows transactional exchanges and aims to inspire and elevate followers toward higher performance levels. Furthermore, leaders with transformational leadership promote a sense of purpose and vision, emphasizing collective goals over individual pursuits. They act as role models, showcasing the strength and resilience associated with the divine masculine while fostering empathy and compassion.

Within the divine masculine framework, transformational leaders leverage strength to inspire change, vision to guide transformation, and empathy to connect with and understand the needs of their team. Transformational leadership is an excellent example of harmonious synergy between the elements of divine masculine energy and effective leadership.

Servant Leadership

Servant leadership, rooted in the idea of leaders serving their teams, resonates strongly with divine masculine principles. Leaders embracing this style prioritize the well-being and growth of their team members with humility and empathy. Servant leaders recognize that true strength lies in empowering others, and true vision encompasses a collective journey toward success.

A servant leader draws strength from their ability to support, guide, and uplift others. This leadership style aligns with the concept of the divine masculine as a force that nurtures and protects, creating a balanced and inclusive environment where everyone feels valued.

Creating a Balance

Leaders aspiring to embody the divine masculine principles must strike a balance between strength, vision, and compassion. Strength in this context is about being resilient when facing challenges and steadfast in achieving a shared vision. Likewise, the vision leaders will set goals and inspire others to see and believe in the larger purpose. Compassion, rooted in empathy, is the glue that will bind the team together, promoting trust and collaboration.

Leaders who successfully integrate these elements create a dynamic and supportive organizational culture. They recognize that the divine masculine is not about dominance but about harmonizing power and compassion, strength and vulnerability, and vision and empathy. Leaders with this mindset can become catalysts for positive change, shaping environments where individuals can thrive, contribute meaningfully, and collectively achieve their highest potential.

Leadership as a Divine Masculine

The emphasis here is not on asserting dominance or control but on empowering others to rise and shine. The divine masculine leader operates from a position of strength, not to overpower others but to provide the necessary support and guidance, helping their peers and subordinates reach their full potential. Here are key aspects of how the divine masculine leader empowers others:

Supportive Guidance

Instead of micromanaging or imposing control, the divine masculine leader offers supportive guidance. This involves providing a framework for growth and success, allowing individuals the autonomy to navigate their path while offering assistance and wisdom when needed. The leader acts as a mentor and ally, creating an environment where each team member feels encouraged to explore their capabilities.

Fostering Collaboration

Instead of enforcing a hierarchical structure, the divine masculine leader promotes collaboration. The focus is on building a collective vision where each person's contributions are valued. This collaborative approach harnesses the diverse talents within the team.

Nurturing Potential

Divine masculine leadership is committed to nurturing the potential within each individual. Leaders focus on understanding team members' unique talents and aspirations and work towards creating opportunities for them to shine. This approach inspires a sense of purpose and fulfillment, as team members are encouraged to express their full potential within the organizational context.

Cultivating a Growth Mindset

Divine masculine leadership promotes a growth mindset within the team. Instead of focusing on fixed roles or limitations, the leader encourages a mindset of continuous learning and improvement. This perspective creates a culture where individuals realize their evolving potential and harness the courage to face challenges.

Case Studies

While it's challenging to definitively attribute success to the embodiment of specific divine masculine qualities, some leaders exhibit characteristics aligned with the principles of strength, vision, compassion, and empowerment. Here are a few examples:

Nelson Mandela
Divine Masculine Qualities: Strength, Vision, Empowerment

The former President of South Africa, Nelson Mandela, exemplified the divine masculine qualities of strength and resilience during his long imprisonment. His unwavering commitment to the vision of a united and democratic South Africa, despite immense personal sacrifice, showcased visionary leadership. After his release, Mandela focused on the divine masculine abilities of reconciliation and empowerment, promoting unity and steering the nation towards a new era.

Mahatma Gandhi
Divine Masculine Qualities: Vision, Compassion, Empowerment

Mahatma Gandhi was a famous leader of India's non-violent independence movement who portrayed divine masculine qualities of compassion and empowerment. His vision for a free and united India inspired millions to join the struggle for independence. Gandhi's leadership was fueled by a profound empathy for the oppressed and a commitment to non-violent resistance.

Martin Luther King Jr.
Divine Masculine Qualities: Vision, Empowerment, Strength

Martin Luther King Jr. was a prominent leader in the American civil rights movement with divine masculine qualities, advocated for equality, and showed strength in the face of adversity. His famous "I Have a Dream" speech articulated a vision of a racially integrated and harmonious America. King's leadership strengthened marginalized communities, contributing to significant societal changes and inspiring future leaders globally.

Elon Musk
Divine Masculine Qualities: Vision, Innovation

Elon Musk, CEO of SpaceX and Tesla, exemplifies divine masculine qualities through his visionary approach to technology and innovation. His bold vision of colonizing Mars with SpaceX and transforming the automotive industry with Tesla demonstrates a commitment to transformative goals. His leadership style empowers his teams to pursue ambitious projects, promoting a culture of innovation and pushing the boundaries of what is possible.

Oprah Winfrey
Divine Masculine Qualities: Compassion, Empowerment, Vision

She is a well-known media personality and philanthropist with divine masculine compassion and empowering leadership qualities. Her inspiring and uplifting energy for media has shaped her successful career. Winfrey's leadership extends beyond her media empire, as she has used her influence to kickstart initiatives promoting education, health, and personal development.

These examples illustrate that leaders who practice divine masculine qualities can profoundly impact organizations, communities, and society at large. Whether through political change, social justice movements, technological advancements, or media influence, these leaders demonstrate how strength, vision, compassion, and empowerment can contribute to positive and transformative leadership outcomes.

Emotional Intelligence in Leadership with Divine Masculine Qualities

Emotional intelligence is crucial to effective leadership, enhancing interpersonal relationships, decision-making, and overall organizational success. Emotional intelligence creates a powerful leadership paradigm when combined with divine masculine qualities like strength, vision, and empowerment. Here's how self-regulation, empathy, and motivation work together to cultivate divine masculine qualities in a leader.

Self-Regulation

Self-regulation within the divine masculine context involves maintaining composure, resilience, and steadiness in the face of challenges. A leader with divine masculine qualities employs self-regulation to channel strength into constructive actions, avoiding impulsive reactions.

Tips and Techniques

- **Mindfulness Practices**: Engage in mindfulness meditation to cultivate self-awareness and control over emotional responses.

- **Reflective Journaling**: Regularly journaling emotions and reactions helps develop awareness and fosters self-regulation.
- **Breathing Exercises**: Deep breathing exercises can effectively manage stress and promote emotional balance.

Empathy

Empathy in the divine masculine leadership context is about understanding the needs and concerns of others while maintaining strength and support. A leader with divine masculine qualities uses empathy to connect with team members and promote a collaborative and supportive environment.

Tips and Techniques

- **Active Listening**: Practice attentive and empathetic listening to fully understand others' perspectives.
- **Seeking Feedback**: Actively seek feedback from team members to understand their experiences and viewpoints.
- **Put Yourself in Others' Shoes**: Develop the habit of considering situations from others' perspectives to enhance empathetic understanding.

Motivation

In the divine masculine leadership framework, motivation involves inspiring others toward a shared vision. A leader with divine masculine qualities leverages motivation to energize the team, aligning their efforts with a higher purpose.

Tips and Techniques

- **Clarify Personal Values**: Align personal values with organizational goals to fuel intrinsic motivation.
- **Set Inspiring Goals**: Establish challenging yet achievable goals that resonate with the team's sense of purpose.
- **Celebrate Achievements**: Acknowledge and celebrate individual and team accomplishments to sustain motivation.

Integration of Traits

Emotionally intelligent leaders with divine masculine qualities strike a balance between strength and sensitivity. They use their strength to provide support and empowerment, while their emotional intelligence enables them to navigate complex interpersonal dynamics with empathy and understanding. These leaders combine their visionary mindset with empathy, ensuring that their strategic decisions consider the well-being and perspectives of their team members. They communicate the larger vision in a way that resonates emotionally, inspiring commitment and collaboration.

Challenges and Growth

A leader with divine masculine qualities and high emotional intelligence recognizes the strength in vulnerability. They acknowledge their own emotions and vulnerabilities, creating an authentic connection with their team. Achieving and maintaining emotional intelligence is an ongoing process. Leaders with divine masculine qualities are committed to continuous self-reflection, learning, and growth, recognizing that emotional intelligence is a dynamic skill that evolves over time.

Effective Communication Strategies

Clarity in Expression

Effective communication begins with clarity in expression, a fundamental trait of divine masculine leadership. Leaders in this paradigm value straightforward messaging, aiming to convey information clearly and directly. This approach reduces the likelihood of misunderstandings and ensures that the entire team shares a common understanding of organizational goals. Leaders often use concrete examples to illustrate points to achieve this clarity, making communication more tangible and accessible to team members.

Assertiveness with Respect

Divine masculine leaders communicate with a unique blend of confidence and respect. Assertiveness is key to their communication style, inspiring trust and decisiveness. However, this assertiveness is balanced with a commitment to active listening, demonstrating genuine interest in others' perspectives.

Alignment with Vision

Alignment with the overarching vision is a critical dimension of divine masculine communication. Leaders ensure that every message, whether conveyed in team meetings or written communications, is consistent with the larger purpose and goals of the organization. This consistency reinforces the shared vision and enhances the team's commitment to it. Also, leaders actively connect day-to-day actions to the overarching vision, clarifying how specific tasks contribute to the realization of shared organizational goals.

Openness to Dialogue

Openness to dialogue is a hallmark of divine masculine communication. Leaders encourage open and constructive dialogue within the team. Addressing challenges directly and constructively is prioritized, as divine masculine leaders understand that facing conflicts head-on contributes to the overall strength and resilience of the team.

Empowering Language

Empowering language is a key aspect of divine masculine communication. Leaders use inclusive pronouns and avoid language that may create a sense of hierarchy or exclusion. Instead, they choose pronouns that emphasize collective ownership and shared responsibility. Regularly acknowledging and appreciating the contributions of team members is a standard practice.

Adaptability in Communication

Adaptability in communication is also emphasized within the divine masculine leadership approach. Leaders recognize that different individuals may respond to communication styles differently. They tailor their approach to suit the needs and preferences of various team members. Establishing feedback loops is essential to ensure that communication remains effective, with ongoing encouragement for team members to provide feedback on communication processes.

Inspiring through Storytelling

Inspiring through storytelling is a powerful divine masculine communication strategy. Leaders craft compelling narratives illustrating the journey, challenges, and triumphs aligned with the shared vision. Storytelling engages emotions, making the message more memorable and inspiring for the team. When appropriate, connecting on a human level by sharing personal stories and experiences humanizes leadership and builds trust.

Setting Expectations

Setting expectations is integral to divine masculine communication. Leaders set clear expectations for their team, communicating roles, responsibilities, and goals with transparency. This clarity prevents misunderstandings and ensures everyone is aligned with the vision and purpose. Regular updates on progress toward goals reinforce the connection between individual efforts and the larger vision.

Incorporating these communication strategies enhances divine masculine qualities in leadership and contributes to the overall effectiveness of communication, fostering a positive and empowered organizational culture.

Chapter 7: Enhancing the Connection: Meditation

The divine masculine is always functioning inside of you. However, there may be interference with the connection, like the static you hear when the signal is bad on the phone. Much like when you want to get a stronger connection on a phone call, you need to shift your position to hear the sacred masculine more clearly. Unlike with the phone, this movement does not happen in the physical, but it occurs in the mind. Meditation is the pathway to shifting the position of the mind.

Meditation is the pathway to shifting the position of the mind.[51]

Mindfulness practices and meditation bring you into the present moment. The divine masculine does not function in the past or future. It only exists in the now. The barrier to connecting with the sacred masculine is overthinking about the past and future. When you dwell on moments that no longer exist or don't yet exist, it takes away from the action you can take now. Therefore, the doorway to manifesting the divine masculine is the use of meditation, mindfulness, grounding, and affirmations to put you in the position to move forward from the trap of your mind.

Understanding Meditation and Mindfulness as the Gateway to the Divine Masculine

Meditation is a vehicle to navigate yourself. Like with any other vehicle, it takes some practice before you can fully control it. A defining attribute of the sacred masculine is that it embodies pinpoint accuracy. Thoughts and perceptions are the distortions that decenter people, throwing them off from an accurate view of reality. Meditation allows you to realize you are not your thoughts and perceptions. Identifying with the observer of your thoughts instead of the thoughts themselves enables you to control and direct your thinking with complete autonomy. Before you can righteously rule over any aspect of your life by functioning within your divine masculinity, you need to control yourself. Meditation helps you understand your true self to mold what emanates from you alchemically.

Meditation dissociates you from your thoughts, worries, biases, and perceptions so you can align with the person within who is beyond these concepts. When you identify with the distortions of what you believe you are, you are empowered to step into knowing. The divine masculine demands a precise, logical, and constant reassessment of how you function within society. Meditation slows you down to allow you to separate from your functionality and tap into a pure sense of existence. From the foundation of existence, you can start to craft the life you want by ordering your thoughts.

Reality begins in the mind. Think of thoughts as a low-density expression of existence. For thoughts to manifest into the external world, they get filtered through higher densities to become tangible. The abstract reality of your thoughts represents the dark feminine because they are hidden from the world in the womb. The masculine plants the seed of action to bring these thoughts into reality. The unbalanced masculine will bring chaos and destruction, while the aligned masculine will create a disciplined order that benefits you and the community. To align your masculine expression, you go inward to the observer of your thoughts to assess what is worthy of taking action. That is how meditation provides the clarity needed to enhance the divine masculine.

Mindfulness is bringing yourself into the present moment. Meditation techniques can enhance your mindfulness. In the present, you are more in tune with what is tangible because the past and the future exist only in your imagination. Remember, the divine masculine is not about the abstract but what is more solid. Condensing your thoughts and desires into reality through the filter of masculinity first requires a profound understanding of the intricacies of what you think. Mindfully being present lets you see which thoughts are relevant to your current situation and which ones will better you right now. This presentness equips you to manipulate your steps according to the reality you want to manifest.

Meditation and mindfulness put you in a better position to make clear and sober decisions, free from the filters of perception and biases. When you meditate, you realize that you may not control what you think, but you have supreme control over how to respond to your thoughts. An ill-disciplined person who has not matured into their divine masculinity becomes a victim to their thoughts, often taking irrational action that can lead to disastrous consequences like ending up in toxic relationships and, in extreme cases, even taking a trip to prison. Meditation and mindfulness are the hammer and chisel that allow you to carve your path out of the material of your thoughts and perceptions.

Anchoring Yourself to Clarity and Strength with Breathing

Breath is one of the most powerful tools for accessing the portal of meditation and mindfulness to the divine masculine. Humans can go without food for a few weeks and a few days without water. However, you can only go without breath for a couple of minutes. Breath is one of the most potent living energies a human has access to. Breathing is a harmonizing force within your system. Your breathing patterns change according to your physical, psychological, and emotional condition. For example, when you are angry or anxious, your breathing will speed up, and when you are calm, it slows down.

In the Biblical narrative, breath is equated to life because it was when God breathed into man's nostrils that he became a living being. The Hebrew word ruach can be used to describe both spirit and breath. In the Hindu tradition, prana is a life force energy that flows through all things, including human bodies. To manage this pranic energy, you must control your breath. Breath is deeply tied to all forms of spirituality across multiple practices. You can find a linguistic link between spirituality and respiration through the letter "spir" as in SPIRit, or reSPIRation. Your breathing and mental state are intrinsically linked.

In meditation, breath control is one of the simplest ways to promote focus and clarity. The beauty of the breath is that it operates automatically, but when you decide to, you can consciously take control of your breathing. Breath control, especially during meditation, is how you can exercise your focus muscle to bring clarity. The technique of breath control can also contribute to gaining both mental and physical strength. For example, professional fighters learn to control their breath under immense strain to maintain energy throughout their match.

Breath control can start with a simple mindfulness meditation exercise. Sit down in a comfortable position with your eyes closed. Allow yourself to breathe as you normally would for a few minutes while you let all your thoughts drift in and out. Do this until you realize your thoughts are beginning to loop, and the same ideas are re-emerging. Now, start controlling the pace of your breathing by bringing your attention to it. Breathe in for five seconds through your nose, and then exhale out of your mouth for five seconds. Whenever your mind wanders, bring your attention back to your breath. When you inhale, focus on how the breath feels entering your nostrils and how your stomach expands. Then, when you exhale, focus on your breath leaving your mouth and how your stomach compresses. That will bring calmness, releasing all the stress from your body and allowing you to gain mental clarity. Furthermore, it creates a body and mind unity needed to engage with the divine masculine.

Stability is one of the central pillars of the sacred masculine. You cannot be stable when you are in a heightened and anxious state. People cannot rely on you as a masculine support if emotions and frantic thoughts easily sway you. Breathing is the key that unlocks a divine emotional control that releases you from stress and anxiety so that you can function in the calm stoicism of masculinity in the face of all kinds of adversities. The world will throw curveballs at you, but you can knock them out of the park by focusing through breath control. A few minutes of conscious breathing before you decide or take action could be the difference between success and failure.

Grounding Yourself

Everything in creation is based on balance. Depending on how you view the earth, it can be personified as masculine or feminine. For example, in Greek mythology, Gaia is the earth goddess, while in Egyptian mythology, the earth is personified as masculine through the god Geb. One of the feminine aspects of the earth is the soil, which gives rise to all the plants and trees. Looking at it through the sacred masculine lens, the mountains and rocks represent a stable and strong masculine essence. Therefore, you access the energy of strength and stability when you use grounding.

Grounding is the practice of using your body to connect with the earth's electricity. Using grounding techniques like walking barefoot on natural ground has numerous physical and psychological benefits. Grounding reduces inflammation in the body, which leads to pain relief and accelerated healing. It also helps you sleep better, which has the psychological benefits of stress reduction, improved mood, and increased focus at work or in your studies. Grounding is one of the simplest activities to connect with the sacred masculine. All you need to do is stand barefoot on soil or grass.

Grounding can be combined with meditation and mindfulness. Envisioning roots sprawling from your feet as you stand on soil or grass establishes a mental connection with the earth in addition to the physical one that your feet touching the ground create. When your roots spread deeply into the earth, reflect on how stabilizing the energy they pull up into your body is. Meditating on the idea of rooting into physical reality is the mental fuel you need to chase down your desires by working on them diligently.

Everybody wears shoes with rubber, plastic, or foam soles in the modern era. This disconnects people from the electricity flowing through the earth. Electricity is like the masculine form of energy, while magnetism represents the feminine. Therefore, humans are electromagnetic beings. The magnetism within you is to attract, while the electricity presents the giving power. Just like the electricity on appliances is used to bring them to life, when grounding, the energy absorbed through the conductors of your feet is rejuvenating and revitalizing.

The central spiritual benefit of grounding is that it reintroduces you to the planet. Many have been misled through modern systems to believe that mankind owns the earth. This misinformation is done through many blatant and subtle programs. For example, people buy and sell land and trade the produce that the earth provides. In reality, the earth owns you. It is your metaphorical mother. Everything your body is comprised of comes from the planet, and when you die, it will get recycled into other living and non-living things. The Bible writes about how humanity came from dust and how you'll return to dust in death. Similarly, the Holy Quran mentions how Adam was made from mud. The grounding connects you to a primal reality that has long been forgotten due to the distortions of modernity.

Not only does grounding connect you with the planet, but it also connects you to all living beings that call Earth home. The surface you stand on can be followed around the world to any random place on the planet through the connections of organic material. Grounding aligns you with nature and your fellow humans while reestablishing a primordial connection with yourself.

Trust and Receptivity Through Crafting a Tranquil Spiritual Space

Transformation starts on the inside. That is not where it stops, however. Your space reflects your internal being. The inner transformation is the foundation, but what is around you can help cultivate that transformative energy. All faith traditions worldwide have some form of elaborate temple because of the universal understanding that the human vehicles of perception, or the senses, are portals. What you consume will eventually influence you. If you constantly eat junk food, after some time, you'll become overweight. Your mouth is not the only portal into your body. Your eyes, ears, and nose also consume whatever is around you. Having a tranquil meditation and mindfulness space to retreat to as a refilling station can be exceedingly helpful.

Practicing in a space fine-tuned to your personal expression of spirituality makes you more receptive to the divine masculinity and trusting to the changes harnessing this potent energy. The subconscious mind does not speak English or any other language but rather communicates in signs and symbols. Only you can craft a space that promotes the mythos you want to unfold in your life. The symbology embedded into your tranquil sanctuary must make sense to your journey because symbols are not always universal. For example, a baseball bat will mean something different to a gangster who uses it to attack people than someone who plays baseball with their grandfather whom they love dearly. Introspect on the masculine attributes like discipline, strength, clarity, and focus, which you would like to grow in your personality. Now, what symbolizes these attributes in your life? You may be a wrestling fan, so Hulk Hogan could symbolize the height of strength, so you can include a poster of him in your space.

Think of the predominant energies you are attempting to manifest and direct your meditation space in that direction. Use all your senses, like smell, sight, and sound. You may want to include a speaker to play calming, meditative music or incorporate pleasant-smelling incense into the room. If you are religious, you can include the icons of your faith. You can also incorporate drums or sound bowls or even decorate the space with pictures of your loved ones. Some people find vision boards useful, so you can fill the room with pictures of the life you want to live or the goals you want to achieve.

The meditation and mindfulness practices you embrace should also be considered when creating your tranquil space. You know yourself better than anybody else. A mission needs to be completed in this room, namely practicing meditative practices to make you receptive and trusting of the divine masculine. This room is not a "mancave" created for pleasure-seeking and escapism. It is a space dedicated to transformative spiritual practice, so minimize distractions and maximize what puts you on the path to opening up yourself for the sacred masculine to come through.

Don't do anything else in your created space other than your spiritual practices. For example, avoid having social visits in the space or finishing up work there. Assign those tasks to other more appropriate areas. It would be inappropriate for someone to throw a rave in a temple because it is dedicated to devotion to God. Similarly, you must respect your spiritual space and set up strong boundaries for yourself and others. Taking some time out of your day to specifically focus on stoking the internal sacred masculine flames can be greatly enhanced when you have an area to go to dedicated to that goal.

Affirmations to Awaken the Sacred Masculine

Affirmations are like mantras or positive statements you repeat to yourself every day so that you can embody what you are saying with your actions. Your speech is the next level of reality that is a step away from your thoughts. Speaking is the beginning of creation. The Genesis account in the Bible says that God spoke the world into existence. This is linked to the third Hermetic principle, which is vibration. Everything is constantly in motion or vibrates at various frequencies. Your speech is a vibration as well, so it has an impact on the physical world. Hearing your voice confirm positive statements influences your mind to take action to live out the statements you make in your affirmations.

Furthermore, the "I am" before most affirmations is a magical statement. When Moses asked God in the Bible what His name was, God replied, "I am that I am." Saying "I am" brings reality to the present moment. It is not the wishful thinking of statements like "I want to be," but rather, it embraces existence in your current space and time. Affirming through the pathway of "I am" recalibrates your mind to accept the statement as true because everything begins in the mental space before it becomes apparent externally. Affirmations are meant to put you in the mentality where you already embody the qualities of the divine masculine instead of hoping one day to achieve them like some sort of distant apparition.

Here is a list of affirmations that are specifically created to assist you in connecting with your divine masculinity more deeply:

- I am a warrior.
- I am confident.
- I know when to take action.
- I am strong.
- I am dedicated to my vision.
- I am disciplined.
- I am patient.
- I am a stable pillar of my home and community.
- I am reliable.
- I am honest and straightforward.

- I am brave.
- I am courageous.
- I overcome all obstacles.
- I am present.
- I am aware.
- I am focused.
- I am resilient and persevere through all hardships.
- I am immovable.
- I am solid.
- I am a powerful leader.
- I am whole.
- I embody the divine masculine in its highest capacity.

You don't have to use all these affirmations. Pick five to ten that most closely resonate with who you are and what you want to achieve. You could also use the list as is if you feel so inclined. Writing your own affirmations specifically catering to your situation is also helpful. Remember to begin the statement with "I am," followed by a positive and affirming sentence. Repeat your affirmation five times in the morning and five times in the evening. It is best to say your affirmations in front of a mirror. Seeing yourself makes them more impactful.

Chapter 8: Finding the Balance Within

Divine Union of Masculine and Feminine

The common view of marriage in the Western world is that two people leave their parents and commit to one another to become one unit. If you break this down mathematically, it can be conceptualized as 1 + 0 = 1. In this numerological representation of the divine union of feminine and masculine, the male is represented by 1, and

Internally, the divine union is when the feminine and masculine aspects of yourself are balanced.[52]

the female is represented by 0. When you compare these numbers to biology, you find that 1 has a phallic shape representing the male sexual organ while the round shape of 0 represents the womb. When the two come together, they are equal to one, meaning there is no separation or duality. Biologically and mythologically, this is presented as the Mother and Father bringing forth the Child.

Therefore, to manifest anything, you need both the masculine and feminine to be present. If you look at the marriage tradition of exchanging rings, you find the external mirror of the divine union. The ring is placed on the finger to symbolize the bond and commitment of the couple to act in one another's best interest. The finger could be interpreted as male, while the ring is female. The finger and the ring make contact to seal the bond of masculine and feminine commitment.

Internally, the divine union is when the feminine and masculine aspects of yourself are balanced. The simplest way to understand this is by viewing the feminine as chaos and the masculine as order. When there is too much chaos in a society, you get lawless anarchy; when there is too much order, you get authoritative tyranny. Both of these outcomes result in death and destruction. Therefore, to function as a whole actualized human, you need to embrace the divine feminine and the divine masculine.

An egg is an analogy of how the divine feminine and masculine balance should work. The shell is masculine, while the internal contents of the egg are feminine. The important part of the egg that turns into a chicken is on the inside. However, the chicken cannot come into existence without the hard shell of masculine protection. In some ways, the vulnerable and emotional parts of yourself are the most real representations of your being, but to function in society, they must be housed in the divine masculine. The purpose of the divine masculine is to deliver the sacred feminine into the world in a way where it can be accepted and protected. In a practical sense, this means allowing yourself to be vulnerable, emotional, and expressive while setting protective boundaries for the world not to take advantage of you.

The divine masculine is like a container, and the sacred feminine is like water. The water flows according to where the container guides it. Therefore, masculinity is often related to leadership. However, to lead, there must be goals, so sometimes, the feminine water shapes the masculine container like a river carving a mountain into a particular shape. This interplay of the water carving up the land, but the land also guiding the water, is what the union of feminine and masculine looks like. Neither is less or more important, but both are needed for you to exist healthily.

Symbolic Representations of Masculine and Feminine Balance in Philosophy and Mythology

The divine feminine and masculine have been symbolized throughout the ages through mythical figures, deities, and philosophical concepts. The idea is so fundamental to existence that it has been presented across cultures and time in an array of forms. In the Hindu pantheon, Shiva and Shakti have personified masculine and feminine energy. The feminine took the form of Parvati and Kali, both representations of Shakti, while the masculine came forth as Shiva.

One of the central narratives to understand the relationship between the divine feminine and masculine is how Kali defeats the demon hoards led by Raktabija, who terrorizes other gods and sages. Kali easily defeated the demons, drinking their blood and beheading them. However, the volatile Shakti energy got so out of control that it became terrifying and dangerous. Lord Shiva went to calm her down. In her uncontrollable rage, she killed him, throwing him to the ground. Once she realized what she had done, she calmed down to breathe life back into Shiva.

This narrative highlights how the creative and powerfully feminine energy gets channeled through the masculine so that it can become ordered. Another way to think of this is as a child who has not yet been socialized. They will hit and bite others and have chaotic emotional outbursts. Over time, they get socialized and begin learning which behaviors are appropriate. If an adult were to behave in the same unhinged manner as a child, it would cause massive disorder with disastrous consequences. A child gets taught how to channel their emotions and communicate their displeasure in more cooperative ways. So, Shakti, as Kali, would be the raw emotional expression of the child, while Shiva is the order that comes through when the emotions are constrained to various pathways.

The universe is made out of matter and energy. Matter can be framed as the masculine, while energy is the feminine. This gendered view of reality permeates all aspects of life. It is then essential to understand that divine feminine and sacred masculine don't necessarily refer to man and woman. When this energy is looked at through such a narrow lens, it lends itself to becoming offensive or even exploitative. Using the words feminine and masculine are just ways to personify concepts to make them easier to understand. In the beginning, the universe existed in a raw state of energy. After the Big Bang, or the masculine seed, was planted, matter developed as an ordered way to express this energy. This is how Shakti and Shiva work together.

Yin and yang is another great example of the divine masculine and sacred feminine described in an ancient culture. Yin is the dark, negative, contemplative, passive, and feminine. Don't think of negative in a moral sense, but rather like the negative charge on a battery or the negative numbers in mathematics. Yang is more active, positive, and masculine. Yin and yang originate from the ancient Chinese Daoist tradition, highlighting how opposing forces create reality to achieve a union of all. To become whole, the Daoist tradition requires a deep understanding of balance, which its practices and philosophies emphasize.

Carl Jung had a unique perspective on the masculine and feminine because he viewed them through the psychological lens. Jung developed the concept of the anima and the animus. Generally, the persona of a man presents as masculine, and that of a woman presents as feminine. The persona is the mask you wear to fit into society. This masculine or feminine persona needs to be balanced to create an internal projection of the ideal man or woman. This ideal is called the animus for women and the anima for men. When a man has integrated his anima, he will healthily express his emotions without being overly domineering. When a woman has integrated her animus, she will be logical, problem-solving, and driven. The anima can then be seen as the feminine aspect of a man, and the animus can be viewed as the male aspect of a woman. To be a whole person, you must integrate this internal part of yourself so you can express both masculine and feminine characteristics appropriately.

What Is the Divine Feminine?

Without understanding the divine feminine, you'll never be able to grasp the concept of the sacred masculine because these two personifications of energy and matter are two sides of the same coin. The feminine and masculine exist on the same spectrum. To analyze one, you need the other. You cannot understand what hot is unless you have experienced cold before to compare it to. If the temperature constantly stayed the same, there would be no hot or cold. Similarly, the masculine and feminine can only be understood due to their juxtaposition. To unlock your divine masculine to its fullest expression, you must also work on the divine feminine.

Where masculine energy is driven, logical, active, giving, and orderly, feminine energy is the exact opposite: emotional, irrational, passive, receiving, and chaotic. The divine feminine is the nurturing softness and vulnerability needed to maintain healthy relationships. It can also be described as the abstract, the mental, and the internal. You need reason and emotion to be balanced in your sacred feminine and masculine. Human beings are not robots, so they cannot function in a sterile state devoid of passion. The divine feminine submits while the sacred masculine leads. However, the feminine also guides. If you use the analogy of a housewife and a working husband, the wife tells the husband everything needed or desired to make the home functional and warm, and then the husband goes out to work to get all those things. So, the divine feminine are your dreams, visions, and passions expressed through physical actions in the sacred masculine space.

Your dreams can be chaotic. Think about your past dreams. Dream sequences don't function rationally. The sequences are not always linear, and the physics of the dream often does not make sense. However, when you are in that realm, the way it functions is not jarring, but it seems normal until you wake up and realize how odd it is. Dreams are where the subconscious mind rationalizes and analyzes your well-being and different events that have occurred recently or in the past. In the chaos of a dream, deep truths are revealed. To integrate these truths and take action accordingly, you can institute the logical masculine to dissect the dream into parts and gain valuable insight to apply in your waking life.

The divine feminine is loving, caring, and nurturing, but at the same time can be volatile and vindictive. When feminine energy is imbalanced, it can result in instability, poisoned relationships, and deceptive manipulation. The story of Medusa best describes how the divine feminine can get so distorted. Medusa was cursed as a result of an illicit affair with the sea god, Poseidon. Her hair was turned to snakes, and any man who looked at her was turned to stone. Men transforming to stone by looking at her is a symbolic representation of masculine arousal. By getting poisoned by fake love, Medusa is no longer able to maintain relationships, instead taking a monstrous form that breaks all the men she comes into contact with through lustful desire. Symbolically, this can be interpreted as someone who has experienced hardships and trauma, becoming bitter and unable to embody the soft feminine. Their value becomes tied to how they can be used and how they can use others. The healthy feminine vulnerability is destroyed by trauma.

The divine feminine also represents spiritual cleansing. The internal work you require to heal from past traumas gets messy. Therefore, only the feminine chaotic energy can be used to heal you. You cannot reason your way out of the unreasonable hurt you've experienced. You need to feel it fully without any logical justifications. Then, you bring in the masculine energy of order to see how deeply ingrained experiences can be integrated into your psyche to produce positive outcomes. The first step, though, is opening the door to flush out the dirt and grime of the past.

Case Study of Harmonizing the Masculine and Feminine: The Story of Mike Tyson

One of the best examples of balanced masculine and feminine energy is the story of Mike Tyson, one of the most legendary boxers to ever put on gloves. Very few people don't know the name of Iron Mike Tyson. His impact has been felt beyond the ring, making him a household name even among people who are not boxing fans. Today, Mike Tyson has a podcast called "Hotboxin' with Mike Tyson," and many see him as a wise sage due to his enlightening and introspective advice.

Tyson's early life was filled with turmoil as his drug-addicted mother sold her body to support the family and her habit. Both Tyson's father and stepfather abandoned the family when he was young. He grew up in Brownsville, a dangerous area of New York that was riddled with crime and poverty. He fell into the dangerous lifestyle of crime and violence that many in his neighborhood embraced before finding an outlet in boxing. His coach, Cus D'Amato, trained Tyson to be an emotionless assassin, which led him to become a world champion.

Today's kind, gentle, but still scary Mike Tyson is far from who he was at the height of his career. He still holds the record for most first-round and second-round knockouts in boxing history. His ferocious peek-a-boo style and terrifying power demolished all opponents who dared to step in front of him, making him the youngest heavyweight champion in the world at the age of 19. His career spiraled out of control after the death of his father figure, coach, and mentor, Cus D'Amato. His excessive partying, drug addiction, and violent lifestyle eventually led him to prison.

When Tyson came back from prison, he was not immediately reformed. However, he eventually reached a crossroads where he realized that he needed to make a change and address the young, scared, and abused boy who still lived inside of him. Through dedicated effort and spiritual practice, Tyson was able to get in touch with his softer side, evolving into the wise and gentle man many know him as today.

Tyson is a living representation of the balance between masculine and feminine. He loved Cus D'Amato and often burst into tears when talking about him. However, D'Amato trained Tyson to be a savage, and the love he had for him was based on the condition that Tyson stayed committed to becoming the best fighter in the world. This transactional form of love and stoking the flames of measured masculinity resulted in Tyson's underdeveloped emotional side. Tyson never dealt with the trauma of his early life, so he looked for an escape through drugs and violence. It was only when Tyson awakened the inner feminine side to become more loving and nurturing to the abused little boy inside of him that he was able to become whole enough to have a healthier expression of masculinity. He had to give himself the feminine love he had never received from his parents, community, or even from his beloved mentor, Cus. In finding this love through psychological and spiritual work, Tyson could balance the masculine and feminine, meaning that he could do excruciating damage but had the introspective self-control to act lovingly.

Mindfulness and Self-Awareness to Detect Imbalances in Yourself

Much like Tyson had to recognize that the scared little boy inside of him is what led him to express himself violently, you need to analyze yourself to identify which imbalances you have. The first step is blatant honesty. People tend to tell themselves lies so they can meaningfully exist in the world without facing their inner demons, which manifest in most of the problems in their lives. There is always this dynamic of the blame game and pointing fingers at the external world about why things are not going the way you would like them to. If you search within yourself, you'll find why you keep repeating many of the same mistakes and get attracted to negative relationships that bring you down.

Write down the answers to the following questions. Remember to be as honest as possible so that the exercise can reveal some of the deeper truths you keep buried and hidden.

1. What are the three main issues that you see constantly manifesting in your life?
2. What limitations or flaws in yourself have caused these issues?
3. Write down a scenario from the past where these flaws have resulted in a negative outcome.
4. How could the outcome have been worse?
5. How could the outcome have been better?
6. What should you change about yourself to prevent this flaw from continually hindering you?
7. What are your weaknesses?
8. How have your weaknesses held you back?
9. How can you minimize the negative impact of your weaknesses?
10. What are the origins of your weaknesses in childhood?
11. What are your strengths?
12. How have your strengths benefitted you?
13. What are the origins of your strengths in childhood?

Answering these questions will make you more self-aware and point you in the right direction of applying the healing and nurturing divine feminine, as well as the sacred masculine actions you can take to grow and improve yourself.

The following mindfulness visualization exercise will help you balance your masculine and feminine. The exercise will help heal your inner child and equip you with the tools to move forward and make informed decisions about your life.

Start by lying down and taking a few deep breaths in and out.

Imagine yourself in the middle of a cold and windy desert.

In the desert, you find a deep black hole that you cannot see the bottom of.

You notice an old wooden ladder at the edge of the hole.

Begin climbing down the ladder to the bottom of the hole. There is no light inside the hole, and it is completely dark. You cannot see anything, but you hear the faint echoes of a child crying.

As you descend, the crying gets louder.

Eventually, you reach the bottom of the hole, where you find a child crying, curled up in a ball.

You approach the child, who is still a shadowy outline in the darkness. When you get close enough to see the child, his back is turned towards you. You tap the child on the shoulder and find it was you when you were ten.

Ask the child why they are crying.

What did they say?

You give the child a big, loving hug to ease their pain.

The child lets out a joyful giggle.

Now, ask the child what you should do when you get back to your world at the top of the hole.

Slowly climb up the ladder as the child joyfully waves goodbye, thanking you for your help.

As you get closer to the top of the hole while climbing, you see light breaking through.

When you finally climb out, the desert has turned into a lush forest.

Now, open your eyes and write down the answers that the child gave you. This visualization exercise will guide you as to what hurt inside of you needs the divine feminine to heal and what sacred masculine steps you need to take to manifest the life you want.

Chapter 9: Tools for Healing Masculinity

The term wounded masculine refers to the negative impacts and manifestations of traditional gender roles and societal expectations on men's emotional well-being. Adhering strictly to conventional notions of masculinity and portraying qualities like emotional stoicism, dominance, and avoidance of vulnerability can lead to emotional and psychological distress.

Adhering strictly to conventional notions of masculinity can lead to emotional and psychological distress.[58]

This chapter explores and addresses how these traditional expectations can harm you by suppressing your emotional expression and promoting a sense of inadequacy when it comes to understanding and dealing with emotions. The wounded masculine concept, in simple words, means that adhering rigidly to traditional gender roles can create emotional wounds and challenges for men that may hinder their overall well-being.

The goal here is to redefine these traditional notions of masculinity, encouraging a more inclusive and emotionally open understanding of what it means to be a man. This chapter offers practical strategies and insights to help men embrace vulnerability, heal from emotional wounds, and develop a healthier relationship with their emotions. The right shift in perspective can contribute to a more positive and holistic approach to masculinity, improving emotional well-being and personal growth.

Common Struggles

The struggles and signs associated with the wounded masculine can manifest in various ways. It's important to note that individuals may experience these challenges to varying degrees, and not everyone adheres strictly to traditional gender roles. Nevertheless, some everyday struggles and signs associated with the wounded masculine include:

Fear of Vulnerability

If you find it difficult to express your emotions openly, you may be experiencing the wounded masculine. There's often a deep-seated fear of showing vulnerability or perceived weakness. This fear might make it challenging to seek help or support, as acknowledging emotional struggles can be daunting.

Shame

The wounded masculine may lead to feelings of inadequacy or failure, often rooted in internalized shame for not meeting societal expectations of masculinity. It's important to recognize and address this shame, as it can significantly influence your self-perception and make it difficult to embrace your own flaws and imperfections.

Lack of Emotional Expression

If you notice a limited emotional range and struggle to express emotions like sadness, fear, or tenderness, you might be experiencing the wounded masculine. That can lead to disconnecting from your own emotional experiences and challenges in understanding and articulating your feelings.

Isolation

Do you find yourself withdrawing or emotionally isolating? The wounded masculine can hinder the formation of deep, meaningful connections due to the fear of vulnerability and difficulty expressing emotions. Building and maintaining healthy relationships may require addressing these challenges.

Distorted Sexual Energy

Challenges in forming intimate connections are common in the wounded masculine. Emotional barriers may impede genuine intimacy and connection, leading to unhealthy attitudes or behaviors related to sexuality. Transforming distorted sexual energy is a crucial aspect of the healing process.

Perfectionism

If you constantly need to prove your worth or competence and set unrealistically high standards, perfectionism associated with the wounded masculine may be at play. It's essential to recognize and navigate this perfectionistic mindset, including addressing the fear of failure and avoiding situations where success is not guaranteed.

Aggression or Hostility

Have you noticed yourself expressing frustration or emotional pain through aggression? That can be a common manifestation of the wounded masculine. Difficulty managing and channeling anger healthily may result in using aggression as a defense mechanism, impacting your well-being and relationships.

Lack of Direction and Motivation

Feeling lost or without a clear purpose is a hallmark of the wounded masculine. If you're struggling to set and pursue meaningful goals, exploring and discovering personal passions is essential. This exploration is crucial for overcoming a lack of motivation and enthusiasm for life.

Dependency on External Validation

Are you primarily seeking validation from external sources? The wounded masculine often relies on societal expectations or others' opinions for self-worth. Breaking free from this cycle of dependence is crucial for genuine self-acceptance and self-validation.

Avoidance of Introspection

If you find yourself avoiding self-reflection, conversations, or activities that prompt deeper self-exploration, it may be time to embrace introspection. The wounded masculine often involves reluctance to confront and address personal challenges. Taking steps toward introspection is a vital part of your journey toward healing and growth.

The Root Causes

As you read through, consider how these factors might resonate with your own experiences:

Childhood Trauma

The impact of childhood trauma is profound, shaping the sense of self and influencing behaviors. Experiences like physical, emotional, or sexual abuse, as well as neglect, can become internalized, giving rise to negative beliefs and coping mechanisms that significantly influence the understanding of masculinity.

Internalization of Negative Beliefs

It's typical for societal expectations and cultural norms to promote negative beliefs about oneself, particularly in the context of traditional masculinity.

Parental Wounds

The relationships you share with parents shape your identities. Strained connections with your father may leave you without a positive male role model, confusing healthy masculinity. Alternatively, challenging relationships with the mother can impact emotional well-being and affect how one navigates relationships.

Lack of a Positive Male Role Model

The absence of a positive male role model during formative years can leave a void where you lack clear guidance on healthy masculinity. This gap may drive anyone to identify their values in environments that reinforce traditional stereotypes. However, this pursuit can backfire and sometimes perpetuate harmful behaviors.

Societal Expectations and Gender Norms

Societal expectations regarding gender roles can exert significant pressure, contributing to wounded masculinity. The insistence on conforming to stereotypical masculine traits, like emotional stoicism and dominance, may lead to suppressing authentic emotions and developing a distorted sense of self.

Peer Pressure and Social Conditioning

Peer influence and societal conditioning play a crucial role in the development of wounded masculinity. The desire to fit in with peer groups or conform to societal norms can lead to the adoption of behaviors that align with traditional masculinity, even if they are detrimental to emotional well-being.

Media Representation

Media portrayal of masculinity is a powerful force that shapes perceptions. Often, media perpetuates narrow ideals and stereotypes, influencing how someone sees themselves. Unrealistic standards of strength, dominance, and success will only trigger negative behaviors and contribute to the development of wounded masculinity.

Reflecting on these factors can provide insight into your experiences and help you understand the influences that may have contributed to your perception of masculinity. By recognizing these root causes, you can carry on the journey of self-discovery and healing, seeking to redefine masculinity in a way that aligns with your authentic self.

Understanding Your Perception

It's a journey of self-reflection, a chance to untangle the threads of beliefs woven into the fabric of your identity. Here are some questions that might bring clarity to your experiences and, in doing so, create space for personal growth, healing, and transformation.

Childhood and Family Dynamics

Think back to your early years. What were the messages about being a man that echoed through your childhood home? How did the dynamics with your father or mother shape your understanding of masculinity? Sometimes, the roots of our beliefs go deep, and acknowledging them is the first step toward understanding.

Personal Beliefs and Conditioning

Consider the beliefs about masculinity you've absorbed from societal expectations and cultural norms. Have you ever found yourself conforming to traditional stereotypes, perhaps unknowingly? Or maybe you've resisted these expectations by forging your own path. Understanding your conditioned beliefs lays the groundwork for intentional self-discovery.

Emotional Expression and Vulnerability

Reflect on your relationship with emotions. How comfortable are you with expressing vulnerability? Have you ever felt the need to suppress certain emotions because they didn't align with societal notions of masculinity? Exploring these aspects can shed light on your emotional landscape.

Role Models and Influences

Who are the figures you've looked up to in terms of masculinity? How have they influenced your perception of being a man? Sometimes, role models shape ideals, knowingly or unknowingly, and examining their impact can reveal much about your own beliefs.

Peer and Social Influences

Think about your friends and social circles. In what ways have they influenced your understanding of masculinity? Have you ever felt pressured to conform to certain ideals to fit in? The social environment often plays a significant role in shaping identities.

Media Representation

Consider the role of media in your perception of masculinity. How have portrayals in movies, TV shows, or advertisements influenced how you see yourself? Have you ever compared yourself to media images of "ideal" masculinity, and how did that make you feel? Media holds a mirror to society, reflecting and shaping our perceptions.

Personal Growth and Healing

What outdated expectations about masculinity are you ready to let go of? How can embracing a more authentic and inclusive definition of masculinity contribute to your personal growth and healing? Recognizing the need for change is the first step toward transformation.

Relationships and Intimacy

Consider the impact of your perception of masculinity on your relationships, especially in terms of intimacy and emotional connection. Have societal expectations ever hindered your ability to be vulnerable in relationships? Understanding these dynamics can pave the way for more authentic connections.

Cultural and Societal Expectations

How do cultural or societal expectations about masculinity influence your choices in your daily life? Are there pressures you're ready to challenge or redefine in your understanding of being a man? Taking a critical look at these influences can empower you to shape your identity on your own terms.

Engaging with these questions isn't just a journey of reflection. It's a step towards understanding, growth, and self-empowerment. It's about letting go of societal pressures that no longer serve you and creating space for masculinity that aligns with your authentic self.

Mindfulness Meditation

Mindfulness meditation is a powerful practice that can significantly cultivate self-awareness and enhance emotional intelligence.

Understanding Mindfulness Meditation

Mindfulness meditation is rooted in ancient contemplative traditions, particularly in Buddhism, and has gained widespread recognition for its benefits in promoting mental well-being. At its core, mindfulness involves cultivating a heightened awareness and presence in the current moment.

Getting Started with Mindfulness Meditation

Find a Quiet Space

Choose a quiet and comfortable space where you won't be disturbed. That could be a corner of your room, a park, or any place where you can sit or lie down comfortably.

Assume a Comfortable Posture

Sit in a comfortable position with your back straight. You can sit on a chair or cushion, cross-legged on the floor, or even lie down. The key is to maintain a posture that is both relaxed and alert.

Focus on Your Breath

Begin by bringing your attention to your breath. Notice the sensation of each inhalation and exhalation. You can focus on the rise and fall of your chest or the sensation of air passing through your nostrils.

Cultivate Present-Moment Awareness

As you breathe, let your attention rest entirely on the present moment. Notice any thoughts, sensations, or emotions that arise without judgment.

The goal is not to eliminate thoughts but to observe them with curiosity and non-judgmental awareness.

Bring Attention Back to the Breath

When your mind inevitably wanders (as it naturally does), gently guide your attention back to your breath. This process of redirecting your focus helps strengthen your ability to stay present.

Body Scan Meditation (Optional)

Another mindfulness technique involves a body scan, systematically bringing your attention to different body parts, observing sensations, and promoting relaxation.

Benefits of Mindfulness Meditation

Increased Self-Awareness

Mindfulness meditation encourages a deep connection with your thoughts, emotions, and bodily sensations. Regularly observing your mental landscape, you develop a heightened self-awareness, recognizing patterns and understanding your inner world more profoundly.

Emotional Regulation

Mindfulness helps in recognizing and processing emotions as they arise. By observing emotions without immediate reaction or judgment, you can respond skillfully to situations, promoting emotional regulation and balance.

Enhanced Concentration and Focus

The practice of mindfulness strengthens your ability to concentrate on the present moment. This heightened focus extends to your daily activities, improving your attention span and overall cognitive performance.

Stress Reduction

Mindfulness has been shown to reduce stress by promoting relaxation and cultivating a non-reactive awareness of stressors. This, in turn, contributes to better emotional well-being.

Improved Interpersonal Relationships

Mindfulness meditation positively impacts your interactions with others by fostering self-awareness and emotional intelligence. You become more attuned to the emotions of those around you, enhancing empathy and communication skills.

Integrating Mindfulness into Daily Life

Start Small

Begin with short sessions, perhaps 5-10 minutes, and gradually increase the duration as you become more comfortable with the practice.

Consistency Is Key

Regularity is more important than duration. Aim for daily practice to experience the cumulative benefits of mindfulness.

Mindful Activities

Extend mindfulness to daily activities such as eating, walking, or washing dishes. Engage fully in these moments, bringing your attention to the present.

Mindfulness Apps and Resources

Consider using mindfulness apps that offer guided meditations. These tools can provide structure and support, especially if you're new to the practice.

Remember, mindfulness meditation is a journey, not a destination. Be patient with yourself and approach the practice with a gentle and compassionate mindset. As you cultivate self-awareness and emotional intelligence through mindfulness, you'll likely find it a valuable resource for navigating life's challenges with greater ease and clarity.

Expressing Emotions

Expressing emotions healthily and assertively is a crucial aspect of emotional well-being. Here are some insights and practical tips to help readers articulate their feelings and vulnerabilities without associating them with weakness:

Understanding Assertiveness

Assertiveness involves expressing your thoughts, feelings and needs clearly and respectfully while respecting the rights and boundaries of others. It's about finding a balance between being open and honest without being passive or aggressive.

Identify and Acknowledge Your Emotions

Start by recognizing and acknowledging your emotions. Understand that all feelings are valid and natural. Whether joy, sadness, frustration, or vulnerability, each emotion conveys essential information about your inner experience.

Use "I" Statements

When expressing your feelings or vulnerabilities, frame your statements using "I" statements. For example, instead of saying, "You always do this," say, "I feel frustrated when this happens." That helps you take ownership of your emotions and avoids sounding accusatory.

Be Specific

Provide specific details about your feelings or vulnerabilities. This clarity helps others understand your perspective and facilitates more effective communication. Instead of saying, "I'm upset about everything," specify the particular actions or situations that bother you.

Practice Active Listening

Developing assertiveness involves not only expressing yourself but also actively listening to others. When in a conversation, make an effort to understand the other person's perspective. That creates a supportive environment for open communication.

Set Boundaries

Clearly define your boundaries and communicate them assertively. Let others know what behaviors are acceptable and unacceptable to you. That helps with establishing healthy and respectful relationships.

Choose the Right Time and Place

Timing and environment matter. Choose a suitable time and place for expressing your feelings, especially if the matter is sensitive. That ensures you and the other person can engage in the conversation without unnecessary distractions or pressures.

Practice Self-Compassion

Recognize that expressing vulnerabilities is a sign of strength, not weakness. Practice self-compassion by acknowledging that everyone has vulnerabilities and it's okay to share them. Treat yourself with the same kindness you would offer to a friend.

Seek Solutions

When expressing your feelings, be open to discussing potential solutions or compromises. This proactive approach demonstrates a willingness to work together and find resolutions rather than venting frustrations.

Use Positive Affirmations

Integrate positive affirmations into your self-talk. Remind yourself that expressing emotions and vulnerabilities is a courageous and healthy act. Affirmations can help reshape negative beliefs about assertiveness.

Seek Support

If expressing your emotions feels challenging, consider seeking support from friends, family, or a mental health professional. They can provide guidance and encouragement as you develop and practice assertive communication skills.

Remember, being assertive is about fostering healthy communication and relationships. It's a skill that can be developed with practice, and over time, it contributes to a more authentic and fulfilling way of expressing emotions without associating them with weakness. Embracing assertiveness can lead to more meaningful connections and greater empowerment in navigating life's challenges.

This chapter has been a journey into understanding and embracing a more authentic and holistic approach to masculinity. It started by exploring the concept of the "wounded masculine," recognizing the negative impacts of traditional gender roles on men's emotional well-being. By identifying struggles such as fear of vulnerability, shame, and distorted sexual energy, the aim was to shed light on the challenges that many individuals face in adhering strictly to societal expectations.

You've already explored the root causes of wounded masculinity, examining factors such as childhood trauma, internalization of negative beliefs, mother/father wounds, and the absence of positive male role models. Recognizing these influences is crucial for initiating a process of healing and personal growth.

Lastly, you were introduced to mindfulness meditation as a powerful tool for cultivating self-awareness and emotional intelligence. Practicing mindfulness can deepen your connection with yourself, regulate emotions, and navigate life's challenges with greater resilience. From mindfulness meditation to assertive expression of emotions, the chapter provided a toolbox for fostering emotional well-being, self-awareness, and personal growth.

As you reflect on what you've learned, remember that the journey toward a healthier masculinity is ongoing. It involves self-compassion, openness to growth, and a commitment to reshaping your relationship with yourself and the world around you. Embrace the insights gained in this chapter as you navigate the path toward a more fulfilling and authentic expression of your masculinity.

Chapter 10: The Ever-Unfolding Path

The divine masculine does not stagnate. This means that the path toward your destiny in your masculine expression is ever-unfolding. The more you work towards your goals concerning your masculine energy, the more you discover about yourself. When carving out a new path, unfamiliar situations arise. The universal principles of divine masculinity allow you to navigate this darkness with the light of perseverance, awareness, and resilience. The sacred masculine path is a dynamic form of knowledge and wisdom because as you continue unfolding its mysteries, you become aware of how much more there is to discover. However, even with a limited intellectual understanding, the sacred masculine can be experienced through practical application.

The sacred masculine path is a dynamic form of knowledge and wisdom.[54]

The unfolding path of the divine masculine is expansive, revealing new realities that can only be accessed through action. You can use your smartphone to search for information and gain knowledge through diligent study. True wisdom can only be achieved through hands-on experience. No matter how many karate books you read, you'll never understand martial arts until you step into the ring. Similarly, the divine masculine cannot be understood simply by reading this text. It has to be lived out through your journey of growth. The main takeaway that should be highlighted in your understanding of the divine masculine is to stop thinking about it and start doing it. Many talented individuals have been hindered by their fear of taking the first step. There was probably someone who existed in history who was ten times smarter than Albert Einstein, but his name has been forgotten because he never had the bravery to break through the barriers of fear and doubt. Go ahead and dive into the deep end because you'll either sink or swim, but either way, you'll learn a powerful lesson.

Your Personal Transformative Journey

Although the sacred masculine can be interpreted through a societal or even universal lens, the most relevant understanding of this powerful energy is how it relates to you internally. When you are transformed, your actions will change, influencing the community you are a part of. Masculine energy is a seed that cracks open the more you keep watering it with mindfulness, introspection, accountability, and action. Slowly, the roots of the seed begin to spread, and the plant breaks through the soil barrier where others can see the difference in your life. Eventually, the plant bears fruit, which is the point where you begin to reap the benefits of your efforts.

Much like a plant, this transformative journey takes time. Since masculine energy is the process of breaking free from thoughts and dreams into action, it is best to stay focused on the present moment and work on yourself daily. It can be difficult to restrain yourself from dwelling on the past or focusing too much on the future. Mindfulness is an amazing tool that opens the gateways to the sacred masculine. It is the practice of bringing your attention to the present moment by using various meditations and techniques.

Self-analysis and introspection are two more keys that unlock the floodgates of masculine energy. You cannot take informed action if you are operating in delusion. Introspection and self-awareness are ways in which you can be honest with yourself. Part of functioning in the divine masculine is assuming responsibility for where you find yourself and avoiding pointing the finger at others. There is no denying that people and events influence your life. However, you choose how you can respond to these hardships and changes. Responsibility, when you dissect the word, is the ability to respond. You never placed the potholes on the long road of transformation you are embarking on, but you are steering so you can swerve and dodge them. Even if you hit a pothole and flatten a tire, you can pull to the side of the road, gather yourself, change the wheel, and continue pushing forward.

The divine masculine does not baby you to dwell in the self-pity of a "woe is me" attitude. This does not mean you need to cut yourself off from your emotions and become a passionless, cold shell of a human. That is a distorted form of the sacred masculine that is not balanced. Feeling your emotions fully is essential to being whole, but you must find ways to rationally integrate your feelings in ways that benefit you and your community. It does not help to look at a homeless person on the side of the road and feel sad for them. Your feelings are not going to help them in any tangible way. Only once you use the sacred masculine to channel your emotions into action do they become useful in manifesting a better world for yourself and others.

New Insights and Understanding

Exploring archetypes and understanding how they manifest in you both negatively and positively will help you gain new insight into how you function. There is no one way to express the sacred masculine, so how it shows up in your life could completely differ from how you expected it to be. Furthermore, people consistently change, so the archetypes and expressions of masculine energy that served you in one phase may no longer be relevant as you grow. For example, with their battles and experiences, the warrior archetype could gain the wisdom to become a sage as they get older.

All archetypes are expressed in you. However, there are a few that stand out as dominant. Understanding all these narrative forms and the psychological origins that birthed them allows you to plug into the archetypes you need to engage with when they become relevant. For example, you may be working your way up the ladder at your job and receive a promotion into a leadership role. What once worked in your old position will no longer apply to your new one. You may find yourself having to dig into the non-dominant archetypes. By understanding each archetype's ins and outs, you can manifest the new energy needed for any new and uncovered roads.

It is difficult to place any human into a clear-cut box. Most people feel like they are in touch with themselves, but in reality, humans are great at self-delusion. The complexity of the human condition always leaves room for new methods of analysis to be uncovered and developed. Therefore, the tools like archetypal figures used to assess masculine energy are also limited. These narrative structures are helpful, but you should not feel tied to them like a prison. Instead, use them in combination with meditation and mindfulness to unveil the more personalized aspects of your sacred masculine expressions.

The journey through yourself to find what drives you is blurry, which is why feminine energy is seen as chaotic. The process of sorting through the chaos is the masculine revealing itself. The sacred masculine is a ship used for navigating the waters of your being, but the feminine energy is like the wind propelling your sails. You cannot control how the wind blows, but you can adjust your sails to take you in the direction you want to go. It is not always easy because that wind can batter your ship. However, through meditation exercises and journaling, you have to patch up any unexpected holes in the sails to remain on the right path. Sometimes, storms can take you way off your planned route, but self-awareness is the process of recalibrating your compass, checking your maps, and slowly steering your ship to get back on course.

Bringing Positive Change to Yourself and Your Community

The birth of the divine masculine within you is not selfish. When the sacred masculine is actualized, you'll become a benefit to your community and society at large. When you look at what many consider traditional masculine values, which extend out of the primitive, evolutionarily engrained divine masculine, you find that selflessness, giving, and protection all come up as core characteristics of masculinity. Due to the sacred masculine being expressed in the external world, the divine masculine must be communal. Humans are social creatures who organize themselves in hierarchies. The order and leadership that spring forth from the divine masculine must be concerned with the well-being of others.

Masculinity expressed in a self-centered way cannot be called divine. Masculinity should not be super focused on individual gain. The sacred masculine is an energy of giving, while the sacred feminine is the attraction energy of receiving. Its introduction should not strictly be focused on bettering yourself but must also include your role in the community. Essentially, your exploration of self is for you to find out what you deem worthy of giving your life for. This could be your family, country, or a cause near your heart. The sacred masculine is purpose-driven, and humans can only find purpose in connections with others as a social species.

The seeds you plant in the community will come back to feed you. Although you should not expect anything back from selfless service, there will inevitably be those you help along the way who will appreciate you enough to uplift you. As much as an individualistic culture tries to erase the strong bonds between people, the altruistic drive of humanity is deeply encoded into the species' ancestral heritage. Those who have actualized into the sacred masculine are guided by creating a better society for all, especially the weak and vulnerable.

Growing into the Sacred Masculine

Growing and developing into your sacred masculine energy is the most fulfilling journey you can choose to embark on. A life spent passively waiting is wasted. The sacred masculine compels you to go out and get what you want, and in this pursuit, endless lessons will be learned. If you have the privilege of making it to old age, the divine masculine is what shapes the stories you will tell to younger generations – as well as the tales that will be told about you. This is your hero's journey. With your work and good deeds, you carve out the mythology attached to your name for generations to come.

You will not transform overnight, so adjust your expectations accordingly. Take small but consistent steps to apply the plan you crafted with your meditations and self-analysis. It is not heated motivation that brings forward victory but slow and steady discipline. The divine masculine requires you to constantly be putting in the effort, even on days when you don't want to. An Olympic runner trains for years to achieve victory in a few seconds. Your moment in the sunshine will only come about from the dirt under your nails, from clawing to the top when no one is looking.

As technology gets humans away from real-life interaction, an epidemic of loneliness is developing. Connection is what creates meaning. The loneliness permeating Western culture can only be cured by re-embracing divine masculinity outside of strictly acquiring excessive wealth. Playing the game is not just about the points you get on the scoreboard. There is nothing wrong with the desire to achieve, but being present in your sacred masculine energy means savoring every moment of the construction process.

Looking at a tall building and marveling at it is moving, but imagine how it feels when the people who laid the bricks and poured the concrete look at it. The pleasure of a job well done is found in the struggle of the process. Lottery winners are quickly separated from their funds because they weren't earned, but if you put your blood, sweat, and tears into something, you'll appreciate it more. Masculine energy is designed to take on strain and embrace challenges. This journey will be difficult because walking through the mud of your internal struggle is one of the hardest tasks you can do. People avoid the internal work needed to grow the divine masculine and opt to drown it with pleasure-seeking and escapism. However, these short-term solutions to the struggle for meaning will always leave you feeling empty. Divine masculine action driven by introspective value development is the only tried and tested path to fulfillment.

Conclusion

Implementation is a fundamental aspect of the sacred masculine. Now that you are done reading this book, you must take action for the profound benefits of the sacred masculine to start appearing in your life. These philosophies, descriptions, and practical tools have no use if you don't put in an effort. Just go ahead and start. Overthinking is the thief of success. For masculine energy to be effective, it has to flow. You'll inevitably make mistakes, but you can only address those flaws once you have identified them through your actions.

As much as you emphasize the sacred masculine, ensuring that you don't neglect the divine feminine is just as important. The chaotic, abstract, irrational, nurturing, and emotional energy of the divine feminine heals you so you can be functional enough to move forward in your pursuit of masculine energy. Regardless of your gender identity, to express the fullness of being human, you must find a balance between these two primordial energies.

The journey is constantly unfolding. Masculine energy is as infinite as the universe. You can never tap into all of it in one sitting. Therefore, the journey of embracing the sacred masculine is persistent. One of the key markers of masculinity is that it moves straight from point A to point B. However, the energy never stagnates because it is all about going forward and accomplishing tasks, so once you are at point B, there will be a point C to get to next. When you are fully invested in your sacred masculine, you will be internally motivated to keep moving and elevating.

Sacred masculine energy is competitive, but it is key to remember that your biggest competition is yourself. If you spend too much time looking around at what the next person is doing, you will never be able to get the razor-sharp focus that the actualized masculine is founded upon. The universe does not reward those constantly turning their necks to look left and right, but it can unlock endless abundance if you keep your eyes on the target. When a runner is completing a 100-meter sprint, you'll seldom see them looking at their competitors because if they stop focusing on the finish line, they will lose, so always keep your unwavering concentration.

Some of the meditative and introspective activities outlined in the book will not work if you only do them once. As you progress in your journey, revisit some concepts and exercises to measure where you are at. The sacred masculine is rational, so constant analysis of yourself in relation to where you once were reveals how far you've come and how far you still need to go.

If you enjoyed this book, I'd greatly appreciate a review on Amazon because it helps me to create more books that people want. It would mean a lot to hear from you.

To leave a review:
1. Open your camera app.
2. Point your mobile device at the QR code.
3. The review page will appear in your web browser.

Thanks for your support!

Here's another book by Mari Silva that you might like

Your Free Gift
(only available for a limited time)

Thanks for getting this book! If you want to learn more about various spirituality topics, then join Mari Silva's community and get a free guided meditation MP3 for awakening your third eye. This guided meditation mp3 is designed to open and strengthen ones third eye so you can experience a higher state of consciousness. Simply visit the link below the image to get started.

https://spiritualityspot.com/meditation

Or, Scan the QR code!

References

Azman, T. (2023, October 16). Spirit Guides: How They Can Offer Comfort and Guidance When You Need It Most. Mindvalley Blog. https://blog.mindvalley.com/spirit-guides/#h-what-is-a-spirit-guide-and-how-do-they-touch-your-life

Budson, A. E. (2021, May 13). Can Mindfulness Change Your Brain? Harvard Health. https://www.health.harvard.edu/blog/can-mindfulness-change-your-brain-202105132455

Chang, P. (2017, September 9). Why The Imbalance of the Divine Feminine & Divine Masculine Energies Is The Root Cause Of Human Suffering. Conscious Reminder. https://consciousreminder.com/2017/09/09/imbalance-divine-feminine-divine-masculine-energies-root-cause-human-suffering/

Dienstmann, G. (2019, July 13). Types of Meditation - An Overview of 23 Meditation Techniques. Live and Dare; Live and Dare. https://liveanddare.com/types-of-meditation/

Isbel, B., Weber, J., Lagopoulos, J., Stefanidis, K., Anderson, H., & Summers, M. J. (2020). Neural Changes in Early Visual Processing after 6 Months of Mindfulness Training in Older Adults. Scientific Reports, 10(1). https://doi.org/10.1038/s41598-020-78343-w

Humphreys, L. C. (2021, October 28). Duality. God Is Both Masculine and Feminine. Medium. https://medium.com/@laurenhumphreys737/duality-god-is-both-masculine-and-feminine-d45b1e3d31e5

Lee, K. A. (2015, May 25). The 4 Female Archetypes of the Moon (+ How to Work with Them). The Moon School. https://www.themoonschool.org/archetypes/four-female-archetypes/

Louise, R. (2014). Loving the Divine Feminine, Integrating the Whole. Elephant Journal. https://www.elephantjournal.com/2014/06/loving-the-divine-feminine-integrating-the-whole/

Lutz, A., Davidson, R. J., & Ricard, M. (2014). Neuroscience Reveals the Secrets of Meditation's Benefits. Scientific American. https://www.scientificamerican.com/article/neuroscience-reveals-the-secrets-of-meditation-s-benefits/

Sage, M. (2023). The Universal Power of Prayer. Psychic Bloggers. https://psychicbloggers.com/archives/21634

Sears, K. (2020). The Basics of 7 Feminine Archetypes from Jungian Psychology. Kaitlyn Sears Yoga. https://kaitlynsearsyoga.com/blogs/news/7-feminine-archetypes

The World Thinks. (2024). Awaken Your Inner Goddess: Discovering the Strength and Beauty Within. The World Thinks. https://theworldthinks.com/awaken-your-inner-goddess/

Tiodar, A. (2021). 11 Qualities of the Divine Feminine Explained. Subconscious Servant. https://subconsciousservant.com/divine-feminine-qualities/

Tiodar, A. (2021, July 14). Divine Masculine: 11 Key Qualities Explained. Subconscious Servant. https://subconsciousservant.com/divine-masculine/

Yugay, I. (2022). 15 Ways to Balance Masculine and Feminine Energy for Resilience. Mindvalley Blog. https://blog.mindvalley.com/masculine-feminine-energy/

Young, A. (2022). 11 Signs Your Spirit Guides Are Communicating with You. Subconscious Servant. https://subconsciousservant.com/signs-your-spirit-guides-are-trying-to-communicate/

Young, A. (2022). How to Find, Connect & Communicate with Your Spirit Guides. Subconscious Servant. https://subconsciousservant.com/how-to-find-your-spirit-guide/

Alethia. (2018, March 4). 9 Ways to Awaken the Divine Masculine Within You. LonerWolf. https://lonerwolf.com/divine-masculine/

Anderson, R. (2023, July 26). The Collective Consciousness of Divine Masculine and Feminine Energies. Www.linkedin.com. https://www.linkedin.com/pulse/collective-consciousness-divine-masculine-feminine-robert-anderson

Atsma, A. J. (2017). Aphrodite Myths 5 Loves - Greek Mythology. Theoi.com. https://www.theoi.com/Olympios/AphroditeLoves.html

Brett. (2011, October 4). The Four Archetypes of the Mature Masculine: The Lover. The Art of Manliness. https://www.artofmanliness.com/character/behavior/the-four-archetypes-of-the-mature-masculine-the-lover/

Brown, S. (2020, September 1). The Divine Masculine and the End of Patriarchy. Curious. https://medium.com/curious/the-divine-masculine-and-the-end-of-patriarchy-5c1c173f906f

Buffalmano, L. (2020, August 9). King, Warrior, Magician, Lover: The 4 Archetypes of Masculinity | TPM. Power DynamicsTM. https://thepowermoves.com/king-warrior-magician-lover/

Cherry, K. (2022, December 16). The 4 Major Jungian Archetypes. Verywell Mind; Verywellmind. https://www.verywellmind.com/what-are-jungs-4-major-archetypes-2795439

Cherry, K. (2023, June 9). Yin and Yang: How Ancient Ideas of Balance Can Help You. Verywell Mind. https://www.verywellmind.com/yin-and-yang-mental-health-7110781

Complex. (2011, August 16). The 10 Craziest Hacks Done By Anonymous. Complex. https://www.complex.com/pop-culture/a/complex/the-10-craziest-anonymous-hacks

Davenport, B. (2022, November 3). 7 Must-Know Masculine Energy Traits with Examples. Live Bold and Bloom. https://liveboldandbloom.com/11/self-improvement/masculine-energy-traits

Divine Masculine Energy: Traits, Balance, and Awakening - Centre of Excellence. (2023, December 27). Www.centreofexcellence.com. https://www.centreofexcellence.com/what-is-the-divine-masculine

Duarte, M. O. (2018, December 1). 12 Jungian Archetypes. Monica O. Duarte. https://monicaoduarte.com/meet-the-12-jungian-archetypes

Eisler, M. (2017, March 10). Laughter Meditation: 5 Healing Benefits and a 10-Minute Practice. Chopra. https://chopra.com/blogs/meditation/laughter-meditation-5-healing-benefits-and-a-10-minute-practice

Farah, S. (2015, February 4). The Archetypes of the Anima and Animus - Appliedjung. Appliedjung. https://appliedjung.com/the-archetypes-of-the-anima-and-animus/

Frawley, D. (n.d.). Understanding Prana. Yogainternational.com. https://yogainternational.com/article/view/understanding-prana/

Get Enough Sleep. (n.d.). Health.gov. https://health.gov/myhealthfinder/healthy-living/mental-health-and-relationships/get-enough-sleep

Gibson, L. (2022, May 4). Have a Problem? Ask Yourself 5 Questions. Mission Possible Strategies. https://missionpossiblestrategies.com/5-questions-to-ask-when-you-have-a-problem/

Gordon, S. (2023, October 5). What Is Grounding? Health. https://www.health.com/grounding-7968373

Gray, A. (2023, May 2). Divine Masculine Energy Traits - 10 Signs. The Invisible Man. https://www.the-invisibleman.com/path/what-is-divine-masculine-energy

Gray, A. (n.d.). Wounded Masculine Energy and Its Essence. The Invisible Man. https://www.the-invisibleman.com/path/what-is-wounded-masculine-energy-exactly

Harris, T. (n.d.). Enhancing Communication with Divine Masculine and Feminine Energies. Buyfromtj. https://www.buyfromtj.com/blog/enhancing-communication-with-divine-masculine-and-feminine-energies

Hilburn, S. (2021, May 28). The Rise of Divine Masculine. Conscious Community Magazine. https://consciouscommunitymagazine.com/the-rise-of-divine-masculine/

Jannyca. (2022, January 31). Embodied Yoga: 3 Ways to "Listen to Your Body" in Yoga. YogaUOnline. https://yogauonline.com/yoga-health-benefits/yoga-for-stress-relief/embodied-yoga-3-ways-to-listen-to-your-body-in-yoga

Jay, S. (2022, October 4). What Is Divine Masculine Energy + 19 Ways to Awaken Your Fire. Revoloon. https://revoloon.com/shanijay/divine-masculine-energy

JimLockard. (2019, September 1). Root Cause: Healing the Wounded Masculine Consciousness, Part 1. New Thought Evolutionary. https://newthoughtevolutionary.wordpress.com/2019/09/01/root-cause-healing-the-wounded-masculine-consciousness-part-1/

Jones, D. (2022, March 29). Mysticism of the Breath. Spirituality+Health. https://www.spiritualityhealth.com/mysticism-of-the-breath

Levesque, A. (2023, June 26). Divine Union: Weaving the Divine Masculine and Divine Feminine. Chaos & Light. https://chaosandlight.com/divine-union/

Lurey, D. (2014, October 9). The Lover - Archetypes of Men. Ekhart Yoga. https://www.ekhartyoga.com/articles/philosophy/the-lover-archetypes-of-men

Lurey, D. (2015, December 16). The Magician - Archetypes of Men. Ekhart Yoga. https://www.ekhartyoga.com/articles/practice/the-magician-archetypes-of-men

Maden, J. (2023). I Think Therefore I Am: Descartes' Cogito Ergo Sum Explained. Philosophybreak.com; Philosophy Break. https://philosophybreak.com/articles/i-think-therefore-i-am-descartes-cogito-ergo-sum-explained/

Main, P. (2023, March 30). Carl Jung's Archetypes. Www.structural-learning.com. https://www.structural-learning.com/post/carl-jungs-archetypes

McCartney, T. (2021, March 18). The Power of Our Breath. Emissaries of Divine Light. https://emissaries.org/the-power-of-our-breath/

Meloy, R. S. (2019, April 24). Balancing Our Feminine and Masculine Energy. Pause Meditation. https://www.pausemeditation.org/single-post/balancing-feminine-masculine-energy

Mindful Staff. (2020, July 8). What Is Mindfulness? Mindful. https://www.mindful.org/what-is-mindfulness/

Oldale, R. J. (2020, September 2). Psychology 101: The 12 Major Archetypes and Their Shadows. Master Mind Content - Master Mind Master Life. https://mastermindcontent.co.uk/psychology-101-the-12-major-archetypes-and-their-shadows/

OVO. (2018). Brand Archetypes - What Are They? Carl Jung's Archetypes as Brands. OVO. https://brandsbyovo.com/expertise/brand-archetypes/

Raypole, C. (2019, May 24). 30 Grounding Techniques to Quiet Distressing Thoughts. Healthline. https://www.healthline.com/health/grounding-techniques

Regan, S. (2021, February 22). These 7 Ancient Laws Can Help You Improve Your Life & Empower Yourself. Mindbodygreen. https://www.mindbodygreen.com/articles/7-hermetic-principles

Regula, deTraci. (2019, June 30). Medusa's Curse: Greek Mythology. ThoughtCo. https://www.thoughtco.com/greek-mythology-medusa-1524415

Resnick, S. (n.d.). Dr. Stella Resnick Psychologist Embodiment Exercises. Dr Stella Resnick. https://www.drstellaresnick.com/embodiment-exercises

Sarah Bence, O. (2023, June 14). Grounding: Its Meaning, Benefits, and Exercises to Try. Verywell Health. https://www.verywellhealth.com/grounding-7494652

Schaffer, A. (2021, October 11). Analysis | Hacktivists are back. Washington Post. https://www.washingtonpost.com/politics/2021/10/11/hacktivists-are-back/

Scruggs-Hussein, T. (2021, August 17). A 12-Minute Meditation to Set the Tone for Your Leadership. Mindful; Mindful.org. https://www.mindful.org/a-12-minute-meditation-to-set-the-tone-for-your-leadership/

Shambo, S. (2023, March 13). 8 Ways to Develop Masculine Energy: Be Irresistible to Women. Tantric Academy. https://tantricacademy.com/masculine-energy/

Shiva and Kali: The Tantric Symbolism. (n.d.). Isha.sadhguru.org. https://isha.sadhguru.org/mahashivratri/shiva/shiva-kali-the-tantric-symbolism/

Sinatra, S. T., Sinatra, D. S., Sinatra, S. W., & Chevalier, G. (2023). Grounding – The Universal Anti-Inflammatory Remedy. Biomedical Journal, 46(1), 11-16. https://doi.org/10.1016/j.bj.2022.12.002

Spiritual Meditation. (2023, September 26). Www.uh.edu. https://www.uh.edu/adbruce/wellness/spiritual-meditation/

TemplePurohit. (2022, February 3). TemplePurohit. https://www.templepurohit.com/shiva-shakti-divine-union-consciousness-energy/

The Holy Bible, New International Version. (1984). Grand Rapids: Zondervan Publishing House

Wong, C. (2021, April 8). Mindfulness Meditation. Verywell Mind; Verywellmind. https://www.verywellmind.com/mindfulness-meditation-88369

You Struggle to Sit Still. (2022, October 3). The Times of India. https://timesofindia.indiatimes.com/life-style/relationships/love-sex/signs-your-masculinity-is-wounded/photostory/94539880.cms?picid=94539905

Your Headspace Mindfulness & Meditation Experts. (2023, October 13). What Is a Flow State, and What Are Its Benefits? Headspace. https://www.headspace.com/articles/flow-state

Yuan, L. (2022, January 3). Guide: 12 Jungian Archetypes as Popularized by the Hero and the Outlaw | Personality Psychology. Personality-Psychology.com. https://personality-psychology.com/guide-12-jungian-archetypes/

Image Sources

[1] https://www.pexels.com/photo/light-man-people-woman-6932056/

[2] *Jakub Hałun, CC BY-SA 4.0 <https://creativecommons.org/licenses/by-sa/4.0>, via Wikimedia Commons* https://commons.wikimedia.org/wiki/File:Venus_of_Willendorf,_20210730_1214_1255.jpg

[3] *Hamelin de Guettelet, CC BY-SA 3.0 <https://creativecommons.org/licenses/by-sa/3.0>, via Wikimedia Commons* https://commons.wikimedia.org/wiki/File:Sleeping_Lady_Hal_Saflieni.jpg

[4] *Zde, CC BY-SA 3.0 <https://creativecommons.org/licenses/by-sa/3.0>, via Wikimedia Commons:* https://commons.wikimedia.org/wiki/File:Cycladic_female_figurine_2800-2300_BC,_AM_Naxos,_143160.jpg

[5] https://commons.wikimedia.org/wiki/File:Simplified-stylized_Minoan_snake_goddess_symbol.svg

[6] *Eternal Space, CC BY-SA 4.0 <https://creativecommons.org/licenses/by-sa/4.0>, via Wikimedia Commons:* https://commons.wikimedia.org/wiki/File:Maat_(Goddess).png

[7] https://www.pexels.com/photo/a-multiple-exposure-photography-of-a-woman-in-black-leather-top-7676532/

[8] https://pixabay.com/photos/woman-scandinavian-young-face-7708174/

[9] https://pixabay.com/photos/pregnant-woman-belly-mother-parent-6178270/

[10] https://pixabay.com/photos/pink-hair-hairstyle-woman-makeup-1450045/

[11] https://pixabay.com/photos/old-woman-veiled-woman-veil-turkey-4189578/

[12] https://commons.wikimedia.org/wiki/File:Jacqueline_Kennedy_in_Venezuela_crop.jpg

[13] https://commons.wikimedia.org/wiki/File:George_Charles_Beresford_-_Virginia_Woolf_in_1902.jpg

[14] https://www.pexels.com/photo/woman-in-white-dress-sitting-on-stone-bench-12506197/

[15] https://www.pexels.com/photo/woman-meditating-with-candles-and-incense-3822864/

[16] https://www.pexels.com/photo/woman-standing-in-one-foot-on-table-170750/
[17] https://www.pexels.com/photo/a-woman-doing-nostril-breathing-6648567/
[18] https://www.pexels.com/photo/elderly-woman-writing-her-diary-while-smiling-7260644/
[19] https://pixabay.com/photos/book-cover-holy-spiritual-light-4393603/
[20] https://www.wallpaperflare.com/owls-pharaoh-eagle-owl-eyes-bird-one-animal-animal-wildlife-wallpaper-warod
[21] https://unsplash.com/photos/brown-fox-on-snow-field-xUUZcpQlqpM?utm_content=creditShareLink&utm_medium=referral&utm_source=unsplash
[22] https://www.pexels.com/photo/woman-meditating-in-the-outdoors-2908175/
[23] Pinterpandai.com, CC BY-SA 3.0 <https://creativecommons.org/licenses/by-sa/3.0>, via Wikimedia Commons: https://commons.wikimedia.org/wiki/File:333_Angel_Number.jpg
[24] https://pixabay.com/photos/magical-woman-fantasy-creative-6046020/
[25] https://unsplash.com/photos/the-big-bang-theory-dvd-Lh3cimWevas?utm_content=creditShareLink&utm_medium=referral&utm_source=unsplash
[26] https://pixabay.com/photos/meditate-woman-yoga-zen-meditating-1851165/
[27] https://pixabay.com/photos/hands-body-woman-posture-hand-5037846/
[28] Elperrofeliz345678, CC BY-SA 4.0 <https://creativecommons.org/licenses/by-sa/4.0>, via Wikimedia Commons: https://commons.wikimedia.org/wiki/File:Abrahamic_religions.png
[29] https://pixabay.com/photos/horoscope-fate-goddess-space-7650723/
[30] Photo by Edz Norton on Unsplash https://unsplash.com/photos/text-j5itydU55FI
[31] https://www.pexels.com/photo/silhouette-of-2-person-standing-in-front-of-white-and-black-stripe-wall-6491960/
[32] https://unsplash.com/photos/man-in-black-suit-standing-on-top-of-building-looking-at-city-buildings-during-daytime-5BIbTwXbTWk
[33] orionpozo, ATTRIBUTION 2.0 GENERIC, CC BY 2.0, <https://creativecommons.org/licenses/by/2.0/>https://www.flickr.com/photos/orionpozo/6914204764
[34] https://pixabay.com/photos/alice-wonderland-mushrooms-fiction-6024906/
[35] https://commons.wikimedia.org/wiki/File:Neil_Hamilton_as_Nick_Carraway_in_The_Great_Gatsby_(1926).jpg
[36] https://unsplash.com/photos/person-wearing-mask-flha0KwRrRc
[37] https://pixabay.com/photos/compass-hand-lake-adventure-4891499/
[38] https://pixabay.com/photos/guitar-player-music-guitarist-5043613/
[39] https://www.pexels.com/photo/close-up-shot-of-a-poker-card-5966408/
[40] https://www.pexels.com/photo/a-man-doing-illusion-6255279/
[41] https://www.pexels.com/photo/positive-black-man-demonstrating-red-heart-in-hands-6974956/
[42] https://www.pexels.com/photo/man-holding-woman-s-hands-8127503/

[43] https://www.pexels.com/photo/a-person-wearing-a-jester-costume-6211894/
[44] https://pixabay.com/photos/man-portrait-beard-close-up-old-1851469/
[45] https://pixabay.com/photos/male-meditate-meditation-spiritual-5922911/
[46] https://pixabay.com/photos/fantasy-light-mood-heaven-lovely-2861107/
[47] Gahlotyoga, CC BY-SA 4.0 <https://creativecommons.org/licenses/by-sa/4.0>, via Wikimedia Commons: https://commons.wikimedia.org/wiki/File:Ashish_veerbhadrasana.jpg
[48] Satheesan.vn, CC BY-SA 3.0 <https://creativecommons.org/licenses/by-sa/3.0>, via Wikimedia Commons: https://commons.wikimedia.org/wiki/File:Mountain_Pose.jpg
[49] https://www.pexels.com/photo/man-in-black-crew-neck-t-shirt-sitting-on-brown-sofa-4553272/
[50] https://pixabay.com/photos/mahatma-gandhi-india-independence-2891158/
[51] https://www.pexels.com/photo/man-wearing-black-cap-with-eyes-closed-under-cloudy-sky-810775/
[52] https://www.pexels.com/photo/closeup-photography-of-stacked-stones-1051449/
[53] https://pixabay.com/photos/man-hike-sunset-hiker-mountaineer-1869135/
[54] https://pixabay.com/photos/man-outdoors-monochrome-sunlight-3556090/